Secrets of Corel® Painter™ Experts:
Tips, Techniques, and Insights
for Users of All Abilities

Daryl Wise and Linda Hellfritsch

Course Technology PTR

A part of Cengage Learning

COURSE TECHNOLOGY
CENGAGE Learning™

Australia, Brazil, Japan, Korea, Mexico, Singapore, Spain, United Kingdom, United States

COURSE TECHNOLOGY
CENGAGE Learning

Secrets of Corel® Painter™ Experts:
Tips, Techniques, and Insights
for Users of All Abilities
Daryl Wise and Linda Hellfritsch

Publisher and General Manager:
Stacy L. Hiquet

Associate Director of Marketing:
Sarah Panella

Manager of Editorial Services:
Heather Talbot

Marketing Manager:
Jordan Castellani

Acquisitions Editor:
Heather Hurley

Project/Copy Editor:
Karen A. Gill

Technical Reviewer:
Steve Szoczei

Interior Layout:
Shawn Morningstar

Cover Designer:
Mike Tanamachi

DVD-ROM Producer:
Brandon Penticuff

Indexer:
Kelly Talbot Editing Services

Proofreader:
Gene Redding

Printed in the United States of America
1 2 3 4 5 6 7 14 13 12 11 10

For product information and technology assistance, contact us at
Cengage Learning Customer & Sales Support, 1-800-354-9706.

For permission to use material from this text or product,
submit all requests online at **cengage.com/permissions.**
Further permissions questions can be e-mailed to **permissionrequest@cengage.com.**

Library of Congress Control Number: 2010926280

ISBN-13: 978-1-4354-5720-1

ISBN-10: 1-4354-5720-x

Course Technology, a part of Cengage Learning
20 Channel Center Street
Boston, MA 02210
USA

Cengage Learning is a leading provider of customized learning solutions with office locations around the globe, including Singapore, the United Kingdom, Australia, Mexico, Brazil, and Japan. Locate your local office at: **international.cengage.com/region.**

Cengage Learning products are represented in Canada by Nelson Education, Ltd.

For your lifelong learning solutions, visit **courseptr.com.**

Visit our corporate Web site at **cengage.com.**

Dedicated to the memory of Tom Hedges.

ACKNOWLEDGMENTS

From Daryl Wise

I would like to acknowledge the following individuals who helped make this book possible. First, I need to sincerely thank the creative, passionate, and talented artists who agreed to participate in this book.

I want to thank my dear friend and book partner, Linda Hellfritsch. She worked closely with the editors on every detail of the book and kept the book (and me) on track. She worked long hours to make everything "just right." Her graphics and art background combined with her creative eye for style gave the book its "pop." And her mastery of the English language made the book easy to read and understand.

Thank you to my friends and colleagues at Fractal Design and those I met while working for the company. Because of Painter, I have been fortunate to cross paths with so many interesting and creative people! Although they are no longer with us, I want to acknowledge Bob Lansdon and Karena Vance—I cherish the time I spent with them.

Also, I want to thank the team from Cengage Learning who steered us in the right direction throughout the entire book-writing process: acquisitions editor, Heather Hurley; project and copy editor, Karen Gill; layout tech, Shawn Morningstar; proof-reader, Gene Redding; indexer, Kelly Talbot; and DVD creator, Brandon Penticuff.

Thank you to Corel Painter's product manager, Rob MacDonald, and Steve Szoczei, our tech editor.

And, of course, thanks to Mark Zimmer and Tom Hedges for creating an amazing product! I was fortunate to have worked at Fractal Design for years, and as anyone who worked on Painter will tell you, "It was a heck of a ride!" Painter gave me my professional start in public relations and marketing, and more importantly, my launch into the computer graphics community. I am sorry though that my good friend, Tom Hedges, will not see this book. I know he would have really liked it!

From Linda Hellfritsch

To begin with, I want to sincerely thank all the artists who have agreed to be featured in this book. Thank you for sharing the wonderful artwork, tips, techniques, and insights contained in these pages. Each of you has generously contributed a great deal of time, effort, and patience to prepare answers to our questions, write tutorials, and make screen shots to illustrate your techniques. Through your words, I feel as if I have come to know each of you in a personal way, and I have thoroughly enjoyed myself as I worked through each and every tutorial during the writing of this book. Without your generous contributions of time, effort, and artwork, this book would not have been possible.

Thank you to my close friend Daryl for inviting me to coauthor this book. Your passion for digital art, along with your unwavering vision, has been a motivating force in making this book a reality. I am thrilled to be a part of this with you.

Thank you to Karen Gill, the best editor in the world. I am deeply grateful for all that I have learned from you. Thank you for your continued patience with all my questions as I learned the ropes. Working with you has been an absolute joy! Thanks, too, to the rest of the team at Cengage Learning for believing in this project, and to Steve Szoczei, at Corel, for his technical supervision.

Thank you to Jesse DeRooy, my wonderful, fun friend. Your advice and support have been invaluable to my understanding of the book-writing process.

To my family and friends, thank you for the continuing encouragement and support that you have provided over the many months that this book has taken to complete. You have kept me smiling and forced me to take much-needed breaks from working at the computer. And a very special thank you to Tanner for bringing me dinners at my computer, giving me shoulder rubs as I worked, and for taking the awesome picture of Daryl and me.

CHAPTER 3: Richard Swiatlowski

CHAPTER 4: Song Yang

CHAPTER 11: Torsten Wolber

CHAPTER 12: Jean-Luc Touillon

CHAPTER 15: Dwayne Vance

CHAPTER 16: John Derry

Daryl Wise has worked for the past 15 years as the owner/operator of StreetWise PR, a small public relations and marketing firm near the Silicon Valley. Some clients include or have included Macworld Expos, the artist Peter Max, HP, Ambient Design, Adesso, Pixelmator, GLUON, and e frontier. He was director of the Santa Cruz Digital Arts Festival for three years and is a member of Cabrillo College's Digital Arts Advisory Committee. He is the author of *Secrets of Award-Winning Digital Artists* (Wiley) as well as *Secrets of Poser Experts* (Course Technology PTR).

Linda Hellfritsch holds degrees in traditional art and graphic design. She is a fine artist, freelance commercial artist, Web designer, and writer living in La Selva Beach, California. She has curated and hung both traditional and digital art exhibitions in San Jose, San Francisco, Monterey, San Clemente, and Santa Cruz. Her areas of expertise include art, design, art history, and arts education. Linda works primarily with traditional mixed media, although her work has required her to design and develop digital graphic arts products. This exposure to digitally produced art has awakened her curiosity and hunger to learn more about digital art tools. She has spent the past several years talking to digital artists, experiencing their work, and learning their secrets. Linda's background in traditional fine art gives her a unique perspective as a traditional artist in a digital world. In her spare time, she works as a scenic painter and props builder at the new Crocker Theater in Aptos, California.

Daryl and Linda.

Secrets of Corel Painter Experts will give you both technical and creative insights into the artistic working processes of some of today's top artists, illustrators, designers, and photographers working with digital art tools.

Painter software has been on the market for more than 20 years, and some of the experts featured in this book have been using it since it first became available. The collective wisdom and experience of all the artists featured in this book make for a powerful resource and instructional guide. We hope that you will find this book to be not only educational and enjoyable, but inspiring as well.

—Daryl and Linda

What You'll Find in This Book

The concept for this book is to give you the feeling of being inside the personal studio of each expert profiled in these pages. The chapters are designed as a conversation with the artist about an individual creative process. You'll learn their answers to questions and see detailed, step-by-step techniques demonstrated. Each chapter features incredible artwork accompanied by background text and illustrations, all relating to Painter.

Who This Book Is For

This book was created as a way to help you learn from Painter experts, regardless of your skill level. It is for artists, non artists, and art lovers. It is for not only all Painter and other graphics software users—from the beginner to the professional—but traditional artists and those who aspire to become artists. Although this book contains in-depth technical information that is useful for professionals and expert digital artists, it also has simple step-by-step techniques and information that will be useful for hobbyists, novices, and traditional artists looking to explore another medium.

How This Book Is Organized

This book is organized into chapters according to the Painter expert's area of expertise, such as concept art, fine art, illustration, design, and photography. Each chapter details the professional background of an individual expert and includes techniques, insights, and resources followed by an image gallery highlighting some of their work, both personal and professional.

What's on the DVD

On the DVD included with this book, you will find many items submitted by the Painter experts, and by Corel, that are useful, enjoyable, and inspiring.

At the end of each chapter in the book is an "On the DVD" section that lists what is inside each artist's folder. The Painter experts featured in this book have designated folders on the DVD where you can access their image gallery, motion graphics, tutorials, favorite Internet links, and free content.

You will also find a free, 30-day, full working demo version of Painter 11, courtesy of Corel.

Please remember that the artwork, graphics, content, and tutorials are property of the artists and cannot be reproduced without their express written permission. Any free content included on the DVD can be used only for noncommercial use, unless specified otherwise or by consent of the artist.

The History of Painter

by John Derry, Cher Threinen-Pendarvis, Robert MacDonald, and Steve Szoczei (with contributions by Painter creators Mark Zimmer and Tom Hedges)

Painter 1: Natural Media

Mark Zimmer and Tom Hedges founded Fractal Design Corporation in 1990.

Entranced by the new Wacom tablet, Mark Zimmer developed Painter at his house starting in September 1990, and he kept it a secret until late December 1990 when he first showed it to Tom Hedges. During this time, he literally put a microscope to pencil sketches and measured the colors of felt pen combinations. He developed a way for texture to interact with an image through a brush and for brushstrokes to overlay and darken like a color pencil. He demonstrated this to investors in January 1991, and Painter was born. Designers Hal Rucker and Cleo Huggins showed the team the "paint can" package design, and it was chosen for this special product.

Mark and Tom debuted the Painter product at Boston Macworld in August 1991 and hired John Derry at the same show. The product shipped two days later.

The first release of Painter brought to the computer incredibly realistic natural-media tools: grainy charcoal and chalk, felt tip markers that bled into paper, and many other brushes and art materials.

Painter 2: Realistic Watercolor and More

Painter 2 was released in 1992 using a marketing campaign titled "So Hot, So Cool." Whereas Painter 1.0 and 1.2 announced a new type of software to the world, Painter 2 exploded with a variety of tools no one had ever seen before.

The two biggest features in Painter 2 were Apply Lighting and Watercolor, which were then unprecedented in the world of digital graphics. Apply Lighting borrowed from the lexicon of three-dimensional (3D) software and gave it a 2D home. At that time, the watercolor was part of the image canvas, but it yielded realistic results, with the transparent pigment settling into the crevices of the paper grain. Artists saw right away that they could use it both to paint beautiful watercolor-like images and to color pen-and-ink sketches. It was amazing to brush on washes of transparent liquid paint and see it settle into the crevices of the paper grain.

Painter X2: Multiple Floating Selections

The creative team was inspired, and more exciting tools were on the way. Within three months of releasing Painter 2, Fractal Design unleashed an extension for Painter 2. This extension, called Painter X2, was revolutionary because it provided the first commercially available Macintosh-based image compositing environment for desktop computers. The concept of multiple objects was well established within the world of vector-based applications such as Illustrator and CorelDRAW, but no one had ever presented it within a raster- or pixel-based system.

The credit for introducing layers must go to Alvy Ray Smith, who is a true pioneer within the computer graphics community. Most of us are familiar with alpha channels and use them in our current workflows. An innovative genius, Alvy Ray Smith coinvented both alpha channels and paint systems in general. Today it might seem odd to get excited about something so universally employed as layers, but when X2 was first publicly demonstrated, the enthralled crowds couldn't believe their eyes!

Painter 3: New Multimedia and Supermedia Tools

By now, Painter's interface was being filled to the bursting point. As a result, the team designed a new drawer-based interface to contain the art materials, and the new user interface would enable the expansion of Painter well into the future.

The team introduced new multimedia and "supermedia" tools in Painter 3. The team rolled the multiple-selection paradigm of Painter X2 into the program. With the layer environment implemented, it was a just a short step to come up with an onion-skinning feature for animators. Painter 3 unveiled a set of animation tools that could be used with virtually all the expressive media in Painter. Frame stacks, a set of animated images, allowed the frames to be edited individually with Painter tools and then played back, as with a movie or animation. With frame stacks, you could also open a QuickTime movie or a Windows movie.

The Image Hose, a new supermedia feature, was introduced in Painter 3. Many tools in Painter simulate the visual nuances of traditional media, but the Image Hose uses an opposite approach in allowing the creation of imagery

that has no traditional counterpart. In a digital-imaging environment, you do not have to adhere to simulations based only on tradition.

Painter 3 also introduced exciting new brushes that simulated large bundles of brush hairs. With the Brush Controls, artists could now control the density and coarseness of a simulated brush tip.

Whether users worked with natural media, supermedia, or video editing, Painter 3 empowered their creativity.

Painter 4: Moving Along with Web Tools, Mosaics, and Other Cool Effects

The release of Painter 4 in 1995 led Fractal Design to an initial public offering. Painter 4 introduced Net Painter and Web Painter, which were both directly tied into the rise of the World Wide Web. Net Painter took advantage of the interconnection of geographically diverse Painter systems, which enabled collaborative artwork creation. Web Painter allowed images to be saved in the popular Web-centric GIF and JPEG formats and enabled the creation of image maps for use with Web page designs.

With the Mosaic feature, artists could design imagery in the style of traditional tiled mosaics. Unlike traditional mosaics, however, this feature enabled users to clone a photographic source into a mosaic. Individual tiles could be edited for shape and color. Again, Painter took another difficult traditional medium and made it easy and flexible to work with in the digital realm.

Painter 4 also introduced the concept of live free transform using a "reference" floater. Rather than manipulating and potentially degrading the pixels of a floater, a reference floater retains the original image's pixel information in memory. The floater can then be resized, distorted, and so on with the final calculation withheld until the reference floater is committed. The result is a high-quality image without the softness or artifacts that occur with repeated manipulation.

Painter 5: Impasto and More

In 1997, Painter 5 burst onto the scene with more realistic art tools and "supernatural" media. The most innovative features for this release were the incredible Impasto media layer, which allowed interaction with thick paint, complete with realistic highlights and shadows, and the Liquid Metal media layer, which simulated the properties of a viscous mercury-like liquid. Dynamic floaters were also introduced; these were exciting special-effect layers that could be applied to images nondestructively to create other hot effects. Photo brushes made photo retouching easy, and other plug-in brushes like the Gooey brushes made manipulating photos and other imagery more fun.

Painter 6: High-Performance Brushes and a Leaner Interface

When Painter 6 was released in 1999, users were excited about the leaner, meaner interface. Painter 5 had contained palettes that were filled to the brim. In addition to the Brushes palette, Painter 6 combined the controls and the art materials into three expandable palettes: Brush Controls, Art Materials, and Objects.

These new brushes enabled an artist to create rich brush-strokes, and with the addition of color variability, an artist could load each brush with multiple colors. It was also possible to enjoy the look and feel of "wet" paint—new paint that mixed with existing paint as you applied new brushwork. These new brushes also responded to tilt and bearing—new features that were unveiled with the new generation of Wacom tablets. Painting was more intuitive and responsive than ever before.

In 2000, Corel Corporation purchased Painter from MetaCreations and began research toward the development of Painter 7.

Painter 7: Creative New Media Layers and More

Painter 7 was the first version to be completely developed under Corel's ownership, and it presented two new media layers: Liquid Ink and Watercolor. In 2001, Painter 7 was launched at Macworld in New York City, and the aisles of the trade show were filled with excited crowds as they watched the demos of running, dripping watercolor and thick, gooey liquid ink.

With the Liquid Ink layer in Painter 7, users enjoyed painting with a thick, gluey ink medium that was resolution independent, which meant that a small file could be resized without loss of quality.

Corel Painter 8: Efficiency and Compatibility

Corel Painter 8 was released in 2003, and users were enthusiastic about the redesigned, more mainstream interface. Adobe Photoshop users were happy to find that Corel Painter 8 was more compatible with Photoshop. Layers and masks operated more like Photoshop, and it was easier to port files between the two programs. Corel Painter 8 also boasted hundreds of new brushes, organized more easily into 30 brush categories. The Brush Creator made it easier for new users to experiment with creating their own brush variants using the Transposer and the Randomizer, whereas advanced users were pleased to find their familiar brush controls located in the Stroke Designer. Often-used controls were included in a new context-sensitive Property Bar.

Another exciting feature of Corel Painter 8 was the Mixer palette, which users had been requesting a long time. The Mixer palette offered a visually intuitive method for arriving at a desired color or color range. Users could use brush and palette knife tools to select color from a variety of locations and then intermix the colors on a mixing pad. They could then save these mixing pads to and retrieve them from a large library of visually mixed color sources.

Corel Painter IX: Performance and Stability

With Corel Painter IX, the engineers at Corel reworked the Painter code base to simplify, streamline, update, and modernize it. The result of their efforts was a faster, much more stable application.

The most exciting new painting feature in Corel Painter IX was the Artists' Oils brush category. When Corel Painter 8 was released, many users fell in love with the brush used within the Mixer; unfortunately, it was available solely within the Mixer palette. Because of significant user requests, this brush from the Mixer palette in Corel Painter 8 was significantly improved and available as the Artists' Oils brush category in Corel Painter IX.

Painter X: Art and Passion

With the launch of Painter X, the engineers pushed the painting capabilities to a new level. With the introduction of RealBristle painting technology, Painter gave artists the unprecedented look and feel of traditional bristle brushes. These brushes allowed artists to rotate flat brushes and multiload paint on one brush from the mixing palette.

Corel continued to push the speed and performance with this version and introduced a new and improved auto painting palette, which allowed photographers to take their artistic vision even further with the new photo painting capabilities.

Painter 11: Changing What's Possible in Art

The latest version of Painter was developed with the help of the community. The Painter community is a strong and loyal following that had been requesting a number of features. This version introduced a resizable color palette and mixer palette. In addition, the engineers rebuilt the color management tools so that artists would no longer experience color shifting between Painter and other applications like Photoshop.

Painter 11 expanded a continuation of the RealBristle in Painter X with dry media. With a number of pencils, chalks, and blenders, artists are now able to shade with the side of a sharp media when using tilt with a pen tablet.

Final Thoughts

With every new release of Painter, feedback from users has been fundamental to honing and improving the program's capabilities. When it comes to providing creative professionals with a broad range of expressive art-making tools, Corel Painter is still unequaled. With its passionate and incredibly loyal user base, Corel Painter should continue to thrive for a long time to come.

The developers of Painter long ago defined its central theme: faithfully capture the subtleties of the artist's hand for the purpose of personal creative expression. This continues to be the driving force behind both its popularity and its development.

Painter continues to push the creative boundaries brought on by traditional media and other digital applications. Leveraging the texturing and customization abilities of the Painter brush engine allows artists to express the art they have always envisioned. After seeing the visions of the 17 artists profiled in this book, we hope you will feel inspired to do the same.

ANDREAS ROCHA

About the Artist

I've been painting digitally for 13 years. I am mostly self-taught and originally had never considered painting professionally. Art was always a hobby; I thought architecture would be my career. But my love for painting endured, and as my technique improved, I started getting job proposals. I've been freelancing for three years, doing finished illustrations, matte paintings, and conceptual work, alongside 3D architectural previsualizations. I currently live in Portugal with my beautiful wife and my two faithful work companions: a dog and a cat.

Artist's Statement

I try to portray all the imaginary things roaming in my head and share them with the world. I consider myself a lucky person to be able to do such a fulfilling activity for a living.

Influences

My inspirations and influences were built during my childhood in the 80s. The work of poster artist Drew Struzan brings back warm memories of going to the movies to see *Back to the Future* or the Indiana Jones movies and being transported to another world for two hours. That is when my love for fantasy really started. Later I found out how fulfilling it was to be able to put on paper all the things I imagined in my head.

Another big influence is my dear city, Lisbon. It is a city full of variety in terms of architecture, moods, and people. It enriches my visual vocabulary, and I believe my work refers to it subconsciously.

Also, two artists whose work I constantly refer to are Jaime Jones and Khang Le. Their conceptual work is strong, and the apparent ease at which they paint amazes me. The incisiveness and textural quality of their brushstrokes are something I am really inspired by and try to emulate in my work.

ANDREAS ROCHA

Studio

    Software: Painter, Photoshop, Windows

    Hardware: PC, dual monitor 23-inch LCD, Wacom Intuos 4 L

Contact

    Andreas Rocha ■ Lisbon, Portugal ■ Rocha.andreas@gmail.com ■ http://www.andreasrocha.com

CONCEPT ART

Techniques

Step-by-Step Tutorial: Quick Concepts with Painter

The following steps describe the process I sometimes use for the initial exploratory phase of a painting, where I am more concerned about the overall look. My emphasis then is on composition, lighting, color, and mood. Painter is the perfect tool to achieve this with its powerful textured brushes and blenders.

The main tools I use are the Chalk Brush with a custom-created large paper, Just Add Water + Grainy Water blenders, the Loaded Palette Knife, and the Real Pencils.

My main inspiration for these conceptual sketches was *Blade Runner*. I love everything about that movie because it is an absolute landmark in science fiction. What I wanted to capture was the dark mood, the electric greens, and the foggy atmospheres that are so characteristic of the movie.

1. I start by creating a new canvas 2000×2000px. On a new layer, I draw two rectangles and fill them with black. I then check Preserve Transparency in the Layers palette. This setup allows me to quickly jump from one concept to the other while having a frame to separate them. In Figure 1.1, I start with Chalk, Square Chalk and paint some generic shapes. Then I use a custom-created paper with a lot of different textures to add variety to my brushstrokes. The two main colors are a desaturated green and a desaturated cyan. I try to aim for interesting shapes and discover things I might want to portray. Nothing is certain at this stage—it's exploratory.

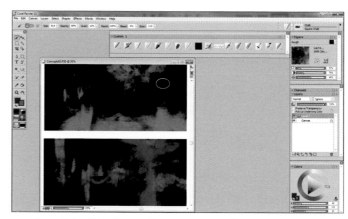

Figure 1.1 Using Preserve Transparency to work on separate images.

2. I pick the Grainy Water Blender and start "washing" over the initial brushstrokes to create contrast between hard textures and smooth areas. Contrast adds interest. In Figure 1.2, I start to see a skyline in the upper sketch and a vertical space between buildings in the lower one.

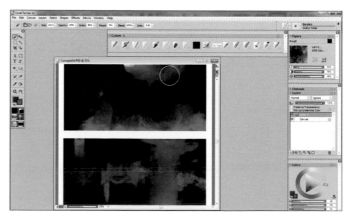

Figure 1.2 Visualize images to define the concept.

3. With the Loaded Palette Knife, I start adding details using warmer colors. These should be small spots of light to spice up the image. With smaller, more opaque brushstrokes, I start to define forms that make sense. I use a zoomed-out view that allows me to a have a clear vision of the image as a whole. It's no use going into too much detail yet. At this stage, I have an overall idea of what I am portraying. In my example, this is an urban plaza for the upper image and some industrial structures for the lower one. See Figure 1.3.

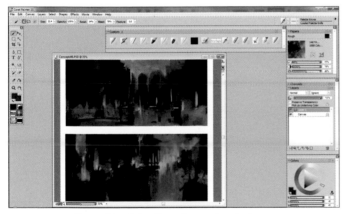

Figure 1.3   Select Zoom Out to view the image.

4. I start working at 50 percent zoom. Using the F-X, Glow Brush, I add interesting highlights around the center of the image. It's important to use dark saturated colors for this to build up these highlights gradually. I try to introduce some different hues, such as the pinks in the bottom image. See Figure 1.4.

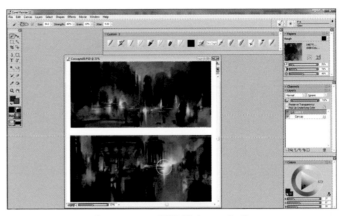

Figure 1.4   Build highlights gradually.

5. Next, I use Rectangular Selection to highlight the upper image and select Edit, Fill. I reduce the opacity to about 15 percent and use a dark green color. See Figure 1.5. I do the same for the lower image but pick a dark magenta. This way I can get rid of the excessive black and introduce a little bit of mood with these overall temperature shifts.

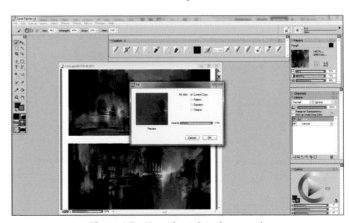

Figure 1.5   Use color to introduce mood.

6. With the Pencils, Real 6B Soft Pencil, I sketch in little figures to give scale and depth. I use the same drawing tool to introduce smaller details like windows and details in the structures. See Figure 1.6.

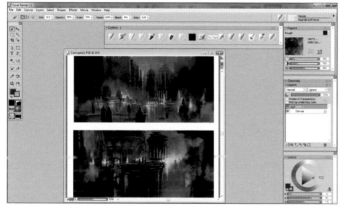

Figure 1.6 Figures in the foreground add perspective.

7. I take a break and come back to the image with a fresh eye. I evaluate the image and am not afraid to make drastic changes to improve it. Now is the perfect time to alter something. I introduce more details in the architecture and objects like the lamp posts to make the image more interesting. See Figure 1.7.

Figure 1.7 Add details to fill the composition.

TIP

Try to work on several paintings simultaneously, because that will help you keep a fresh eye on each when jumping from one to the other. If you are working on only one painting, try not to paint for more than 1 hour straight. A 15-minute break will both rest your fingers and refresh your eyes.

8. Finally, I go to Effects, Tonal Control, Adjust Colors and reduce the Saturation and Value for more contrast. See Figure 1.8.

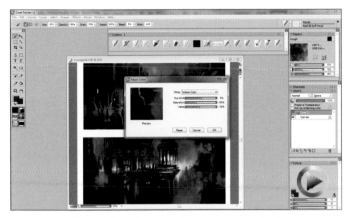

Figure 1.8 Adjust the colors to enhance contrast.

9. In the end, I've got two different scenes with similar moods. See Figure 1.9. Doing two helps me compare various aspects and see what works and what doesn't. The next stage is to further refine one of them or perhaps mix the best elements from both and come up with a new third concept.

Figure 1.9 "Urban Sci-Fi Concepts" final image.

ANDREAS ROCHA

5

Insights

The Creative Process

My initial thought process is actually quite short; I prefer to get paint on the "canvas" straight away. This way I can evaluate what is good and what is bad. I try to be as rough as possible and work in zoomed-out views—black and white is usually the way to go, although desaturated colors follow closely. Once I've found an interesting picture, I resize the canvas to the final resolution and start adding detail without losing my initial concept. It is important for me to take regular breaks so I can evaluate what I have done so far. These breaks also include a good night sleep, which means that when I have the time, I take between three and five days to complete a painting. The more visual breaks I take from the painting the better, because they help me to spot flaws when I come back. Seeking feedback from peers is critical also, because it points out flaws I over-looked and hardens my skin for clients.

Another key thing is to constantly refer to the works of artists I admire. I have a big folder where I keep all these gems, and it is one of my most prized assets. First, I search for artists whose technique and content will help me for a given assignment. Then, during the painting, I try to refer to several works by different artists so I don't become too attached to a particular image.

I use Painter both for my initial conceptual process, where a lot of gestural brushstrokes are involved, and in the latter stages where I need to smooth out some areas and reintroduce texture in others.

Favorite Features

My most adored Painter features are the Palette Knife and Blender brushes. The Palette Knife is a wonderful tool that I use to infuse dynamism and texture. Things really start to come alive when I start using it and, when combined with the tilt of the stylus on the tablet, it makes a versatile tool. The Blenders, on the other hand, have the power to mix colors smoothly and blend the areas where too much brushwork shows. However, I do like to reintroduce some texture by working with the Palette Knife, for example, or using textures with the Grainy Blender or Chalk Brush.

Customizable Tools

Two of the most important customizations I have done to the Painter tools are changing the direction of the Palette Knife to Bearing and making a scan of a real watercolor-painted paper with a lot of different dabs and then using it as a paper texture. This gives me a lot of varied textures, depending on which area of the scanned paper I am using.

Timesaving Tips

The most timesaving aspect of the process is getting to know the program as well as I can (at least the parts that interest me) and using keyboard shortcuts as much as I can. The painting process transforms itself into a fluid motion of brushstrokes where I can almost do things subconsciously.

TIP

I assign four F keys to the zoom commands Zoom In, Zoom Out, Zoom to Fit, and Actual Size. It's handy for me to paint with my left hand while my right hand easily and quickly controls the zoom of the canvas.

Finished Work

It's important to know when to consider the work finished. This is not an easy call. A good night's rest can help me spot flaws the next day. Also, I seek other opinions before publishing my work. When I do consider my work finished, I try to post it on most of the computer graphics (CG) forums I know of. This can be a lengthy process sometimes, because forums have their posting policies, but in the end it is well worth it to get feedback.

Q&A

When did you start using Painter?

I started using Painter in version 2, when it was still Fractal Design Painter. It was already a powerful tool at that time, and the brushes I used the most back then are still the ones I use the most now.

What do you wish someone had told you when you started?

Nothing really...I loved to use the software from the beginning. Over the course of time I slowly learned to know it and understand what it excelled at and where it needed help from other software. This slow learning process was a great way to understand the software and not let myself be controlled by it.

Did you have previous experience in traditional media?

I had no real traditional painting practice. My experience was just with graphite and colored pencils. I tried using acrylics and oils, but I soon gave up. That was about the time that I discovered digital painting. Now I work exclusively in the digital medium.

How has it been for you to learn about using art tools in a digital setting?

Art tools in a digital setting are much more forgiving and easy to pick up. That is one of the reasons for their popularity. Something that fascinates me is the versatility they offer to explore new techniques when trying to come up with new and better results. I'm still in search of the technique that fits me best. I'm sure I will never get there, but I'm getting closer. I would definitely say that my digital art exploration has been a rewarding experience, and I know it will continue to be in the years to come.

What motivates you?

What motivates me is trying to be as good as the artists I most admire. The Internet has such a wealth of digital art content, and it grows daily. Almost each week I find out about a new artist and get blown away by his work. I am inspired by this work and try to emulate the artist's techniques and the overall feeling of his paintings. Another thing that gets me going is comparing my current work to some of my past works and seeing the evolution. This keeps me going and makes me wonder what I can achieve in the future.

Has Painter helped you to define your own style?

The Blender brushes and the Palette Knife really helped introduce the more dramatic aspect of my brushstrokes and make my paintings look less digital and more traditional. I love the way colors are blended using these tools, and I think this is something that I like to retain in most of my paintings.

How has the Internet influenced your art-making process?

The most important thing has been discovery of other artists who showed me how far I can take digital art. This has made me work harder and aspire to become as good as the artists I admire. A daily ingestion of digital artwork keeps my mind fresh and prevents me from getting lazy.

Another important aspect is the wealth of Internet information available on the subject of digital art and all the free tutorials you can find. The digital community is open and, most of the time, ready to help.

What advice do you have for artists working with Painter?

I think it would be to not get overwhelmed by the large array of tools available in Painter and instead try to seek out the few that you can become really good at.

Resources

On the DVD

- Artist Gallery

Links

- http://www.andreasrocha.com
- http://cghub.com
- http://www.conceptart.org
- http://www.3dtotal.com
- http://parkablogs.com
- http://www.cgsociety.org

ANDREAS ROCHA

Education

Architecture degree

Client List

Lego, Phoenix Age, Fantasy Flight Games, Grasshopper Manufacture, ROAR Publishing, Post Panic, Big Tree Games, Radical Publishing, Krypton Photo, American Greetings

Awards and Career Highlights

Graphics for *Castle Age* Facebook game; illustrations for *Space: A Complete Picture of the Universe* (Roar Publishing); matte paintings for *Infinite Oz*

Gallery

"Late Afternoon."

"One Ticket, Please."

"Fresh Meat."

"Padrone e Servi."

ANDREAS ROCHA

"Gateway to Hell."

"Sunset Mountain."

ANDREAS ROCHA

"Explorers."

CONCEPT ART

"The Bridge."

ANDREAS ROCHA

"The Fortress."

CONCEPT ART

"The Waterfall."

ANDREAS ROCHA

"Umbrella Dance."

WAHEED NASIR

About the Artist

I live in Karachi, Pakistan, and have a background in traditional art. My field of work includes art direction, visual development, concept art, matte painting, background plates, creating concepts and references for final lighting and overall mood, and 3D texturing. In addition to my digital work, I paint and hold exhibitions of my traditionally created art whenever time permits. To date, I have had 5 solo exhibitions and taken part in more than 20 group shows, both here and abroad. To cater to my softer side, I play guitar and compose music. I have more than 15 years of experience teaching traditional drawing and painting and guitar. I have more than eight years of experience working as a digital computer graphics (CG) artist. I conduct workshops and give lectures and demonstrations on art at various venues, institutes, and universities. I am currently working as the creative head at Grand Leisure Corporation Limited. When I have the time, I get involved in local and international projects as a freelance artist.

Artist's Statement

I believe art must touch hearts. There must be something more than just painting a beautiful picture—there has to be a story, a mood, and an atmosphere, and something must be going on. Art has to get the viewer involved; it must pull the viewer in and make him think. If it's a painting, it should look like a painting—it shouldn't look like a photograph. One must feel the brushwork—loose and casual, yet calculated. Spontaneous suggestions are always more artistic. Art should be pure, straightforward, and come from the heart.

"Nightlife Cityscape."

Influences

Nature is my biggest inspiration. I am also inspired by the realistic painting styles of the old master expressionists and flamenco guitar music. If it's art, it inspires and influences me.

WAHEED NASIR

Studio

   Software: Painter, Photoshop, Art Rage

   Hardware: Wacom tablet

Contact

   Waheed Nasir ▪ Karachi, Pakistan ▪ Wnasir2@hotmail.com ▪ Waheednasir2@gmail.com ▪ http://www.waheednasir.com

Techniques

Step-by-Step Tutorial: "Those Gloomy Hours"

All the ideas for this image were in and from my mind. My aim was merely to make a conceptual digital painting that had a gloomy atmosphere. I went for a complete shot—showing the time of day (night), strong moonlight, a mountain range, a spooky castle with few lights inside, and water and trees. I planned, and aimed for, a silhouette setting, so I went for a backlit condition. That served my purpose well and was just what I pictured in my mind.

I paint this scene in such a way that it shows details, textures, and light, so if I want to, I can even have it made to use for a 3D short/project.

1. I make my initial sketch on paper using a pencil without references. I visualize the whole scene. While sketching, my only concern is the composition, with the placement of the main mountain and the castle as my focus. My sketch is just a rough suggestion; I am not after details at this time. My objective is to think about an interesting division of negative and positive space. See Figure 2.1.

2. I scan my sketch and open it in Painter to further work, refine, color, and finish it. I use a Wacom tablet while working in Painter. I start by choosing a middle tone— a blue—and add it as a base color to the sky and water using the Pens, Flat Color Brush. See Figure 2.2.

Figure 2.1 Pencil sketch focusing on a strong composition.

Figure 2.2 Import into Painter and begin with a base color.

3. At this time I am more concerned with adding a ground color to every part of the image; I am not concerned with dimensionality at this point. So in Figure 2.3, I use the same Flat Color Brush to add background colors to the mountain and castle, filling these areas with flat colors.

Figure 2.3 Use Pens, Flat Color to fill in background colors.

> ## NOTE
>
> I usually work on the entire canvas at the same time, especially at the start and before going on to the details. I work on the ground, sky, foreground, midground, and background simultaneously. I don't like to finish one particular area first. This technique helps me build harmony throughout.

4. At this stage, I am working to build up the image in various areas, layer by layer, and now want to achieve some dimensionality. During this process, I use various pens along the way with solid, flat strokes, such as Flat Color and Round Tip Pen 10. I play around with the opacity at times and work to create the mood I am after by carefully deciding on a basic ground color for every part of the image. See Figure 2.4.

> ## NOTE
>
> I build up my image layer by layer, in the same manner that I would for a real oil painting (on canvas). This approach helps me achieve a solid, rich-looking surface with body and volume.

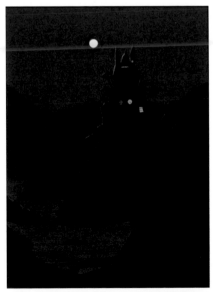

Figure 2.4 Use color to create mood and add dimensionality.

5. I begin adding basic details using Pens, Flat Color for more solid strokes and covering. In Figure 2.5, I add a winding path, which was not in my initial sketch, on the main mountain. It is a major need and a visually interesting choice. This also lends visual significance to the main point of focus: the castle. I create clouds around the moon using Artists' Oils, Dry Brush for my initial swirling shapes; right now their placement is the most important thing for me. I also add ripples in the water using a Flat Pen Brush in a new layer and, for now, just a random suggestion of ripples according to the light.

Figure 2.5 Begin adding details.

NOTE

I would like to suggest that all beginners who want to give digital painting a shot should read and learn about art in general. Besides becoming proficient with the tools and brushes that digital art software offers, you'll have basic knowledge about the elements of art. No tool can make a nice composition for you, tweak a weak arrangement of things, or fix a boring color scheme—you must know about these elements already to produce a solid and convincing piece of artwork. Elements such as composition, focus, depth, perspective, light, tone, color, drama, and mood are crucial to consider when developing your image. You need a combination of tools and a strong know-how of art.

6. Now it's time to make this image much more focused and defined. I start finishing the loose parts, always keeping in mind the light source, which is the moon at the back. Major areas become silhouettes, with light rimming their edges and the parts that would receive straight light from the moon being fully lit. Those areas that fall in a direct line with the moon I make even brighter.

7. In Figure 2.6, I add more details in parts like the foreground mountain. I decide to add branches to the sides of the image in the foreground; I use a Round Tip Pen Brush in a new layer so that I can tweak the shape and positions later if I have to. The branches are a nice frame for the whole view and make the focus even stronger. They also keep the eyes of the viewer inside the edges of the picture plane and more focused on the interesting parts.

Figure 2.6 Focus the image by defining details.

WAHEED NASIR

> **TIP**
>
> Draw with pencils and sketch as much as you can. Practice drawing from life. Learn to make your lines strong and develop a good flow. Practicing these things will give you confidence and make your digital/tablet work strong and impressive.

I also work on the water a little and add more definition. I decide to paint a torch at the bottom of the path on the main mountain. This serves as a visual guide and helps me get rid of the big dark shape of that area. I create the effect of its light with a Soft Pen Brush and make it even softer by blurring it. I add its reflection on the water using a Pen Brush, but I do not keep it as solid and defined as the actual torch flame because it's a reflection, and I want to show the water ripples breaking it up.

> **NOTE**
>
> I constantly observe and judge things while working. I never call any one thing finished during the process but keep working on all areas, all the time, until the end. Even if one part looks finished now, it will probably need attention again once other areas are completed. For example, if I decide to brighten up the moon, I not only add a brighter spot there but have to work on the lighter parts of the clouds, castle, and water—reconsidering the effects of the moonlight all over again, with stronger, more defined highlights.

8. I work to finish the clouds, again using a Pen Brush. I apply a Gaussian blur on the first layer of the clouds and then, in another layer, I define some of their parts and reduce the opacity. The moon is just a circular shape that I make with a Round Tip Pen Brush. To get rid of its flatness, I put a couple of random strokes on it using a darker tone with half the opacity. I keep the area around the moon brighter so that it becomes darker as it gets further away. Even the parts of the clouds closer to the moon and facing it get lighter strokes to show the reflected light. I add additional highlights on the water, on the castle, and on the winding path. See Figure 2.7.

Figure 2.7   Add highlights and reflections.

9. In Figure 2.8, I desaturate the whole image and lessen the contrast a little because it was too blue-ish and too saturated for the eyes. Now it is kind of mature. The desaturation is an afterthought; I make these kinds of decisions all the time —judging, analyzing, and changing things for a better look. I do not have a general rule for these things but always consider what's going to look best. These are mostly under the bracket of "personal taste."

Figure 2.8   Desaturate the image and lessen the contrast.

TIP

Throughout the creation of this image, I did not use a lot of different brushes, but what I did use served my purpose perfectly. Using brushes unnecessarily only makes things look overdone and busy, often disturbing the viewer. Artwork needs to be straight, simple, and to the point.

CONCEPT/FINE ART

10. At this point, I decide I am finished. I choose to leave some areas less detailed because I don't want every area to get equal attention. To become a strong point of focus, the castle and main mountain must be well tackled with all kinds of details. Other parts, especially the mountains in the background, have minimum detailing because I want them to be at a distance, and they must recede into the background; additional details would just bring them forward and ruin any sense of depth. Figure 2.9 shows my final image. Every part works the way I visualized in my original concept.

Figure 2.9 "Those Gloomy Hours" final image.

Insights

The Creative Process

Both my creative process and my approach to art are traditional. I work straight and pure and, to a major extent, I adhere to the basic rules of art. I start by thinking about something specific. I look for a subject that will give me enough creative freedom and a mood to capture—something that will get the viewer involved. For me, this is a natural process. When I plan my images, the most important elements I consider are composition, light, mood, and story. I also want to make sure that I create a visual path so the viewer's eye will travel across the painting but still come back to the main focal point; I love to have a strong point-of-focus for the viewer. After I make my initial sketch, where I take care of basic compositional elements, I add my ground colors and work in lights and darks. I work on the entire canvas at one time because that gives a sense of harmony to the image. I address tones and values rather than colors. I also try to capture air and atmosphere. I finish the image, layer by layer, and work to maintain a consistent mood throughout. Also, I leave many areas in an image unfinished, or roughly done, so the viewer can use his own imagination about it.

Favorite Features

Painter is a beautiful software program that has great features for artists and painters with a traditional art background. I usually use its Oil Brushes, Palette Knives, and Pens; the thick oil impastos are just like the real thing.

Timesaving Tips

I always work in separate layers. This allows me creative freedom and saves a lot of time when things go wrong or need to be changed—which can happen at any point—according to the needs of the project.

Finished Work

I try to make sure that I keep the actual tones, colors, and contrasts and that I don't crop the original image. Also, whenever possible, I like to avoid unnecessary thick, dark framing. The work must be shown with the name and Web site of the artist, along with all due credits. My finished work is usually published on my Web site, as well as in various online forums and galleries. I sometimes create prints of my work, and I have plans to exhibit my digitally painted prints along with my traditional canvas paintings. I am looking forward to finding enough free time to do this soon!

Q&A

When did you start using Painter?

I first used Painter at an animation studio about six years ago. I was working as a concept artist/matte painter and used Painter to paint textures for 3D work. Painter allowed me to create quick concepts for lighting and colors that the art department needed—all the time.

Did you have previous experience in traditional media?

Yes, I have a background in traditional art. Along with digital media, I still work in traditional oils, pastels, charcoal, and pen and ink. My favorite medium is oil paint on canvas. I am a fine artist first, and then a digital one.

Do you integrate your work in Painter with traditional artists' materials?

Sometimes I integrate traditional tools by first drawing my image on paper and then scanning and importing it into Painter for coloring and painting.

How has it been for you to learn about using art tools in a digital setting?

Fortunately, I do have traditional painting experience, so that helps a lot with creating my artwork using digital media. A real artist, with a traditional art background, always has an edge over those who start drawing and painting digitally, with no actual drawing and painting experience.

Has Painter helped you to define your own style?

It has given me those beautiful tools and brushes that are just like traditional ones. I am happy that, even in the digital medium, I can work as a fine artist and create paintings that are like real oils. By being able to keep working in my personal style, I can work fast and even deliver things ahead of schedule.

How does Painter fit into your creative process and workflow?

Painter fits well with my creative process. It gives me the tools to create both realistic work and speedy paintings and concepts for mood, lighting, and colors. I even get what I want for my personal paintings from Painter's large range of brushes.

What motivates you?

Varied happenings motivate me—incidents, memories past, nature, and even a strong piece of any kind of art.

Which artists do you admire?

I admire Caravaggio for his brilliant, realistic paintings, for the way he captured all those moments in time, and for his theatrical lighting. I like John Singer Sargent's bold and casual oil paintings; his strong suggestions and thick brushstrokes are to the point and in the right place. I love his spontaneity. In digital media, I admire Craig Mullins' work.

How has the Internet influenced your art-making process?
The Internet has given me a lot of exposure. I get to see a lot of art by people from around the globe and share mine with them. The Internet has brought me closer to people and allowed me to keep in touch with them. People get jobs and have made their names through the Internet. The Internet can teach me anything I want to learn. It provides tutorials, insights, life histories of artists, and what-not. I need only to have the will to learn, and the Internet is right there beside me to help.

What advice do you have for artists working with Painter?
First of all, understand the interface. Study and explore all that it offers. Get the hang of the tools—there are many—and explore all the brushes to learn which ones suit you and what exactly to use for a particular job. Once you've done that, life with Painter will be quite a lot easier. Furthermore, try exploring the brushes that are closest to traditional media. They're a lot of fun.

Resources

On the DVD
- Artist Gallery

Links
- http://www.waheednasir.com
- http://www.goodbrush.com
- http://www.tinfoilgames.com/
- http://www.dylancolestudio.com/
- http://www.maciejkuciara.com/
- http://www.thomlab.com/
- http://www.johnsingersargent.org/

WAHEED NASIR

Education
BA in commerce.

Client List
MACK/DADD Productions; Sean Kennedy; ICE Animations (Pvt.) Ltd., among others.

Awards and Career Highlights
Cover awards at various digital art forums for paintings and concept work: CGTalk; 3D Total; CG Expanse; 3DM3; cgTantra; ArtRage; among others. Feature/interview on ItsArtMag.com, among others. Work has appeared in various online magazines, such as *2DArtist* by 3D Total.

WAHEED NASIR

CONCEPT/FINE ART

Gallery

"Mountaineers Before Storm."

"Highs and Lows."

CONCEPT/FINE ART

"Honestly Pure."

WAHEED NASIR

"In the Woods."

CONCEPT/FINE ART

"Once Upon a Time."

"Travelling—Old Times."

WAHEED NASIR

"Oriental."

"My Friends."

"Bazaar After Rain."

"True Tints."

RICHARD SWIATLOWSKI

About the Artist

I am a self-taught artist who began drawing while still in grammar school. I work out of my home in Wilbraham, Massachusetts. My signature look is brilliant colors and texture—both in my digital work and with traditional media. I create images using photography, drawings, paintings, and digital media.

Artist's Statement

Color

There's the jumping-off point for me

The wild ride of it

Exciting, pulsing

Pulling me along energy circuits,

Urban scenes, hot pink, searing lights

Waking me up

A paintbrush, a pencil, a camera, a computer

These are nothing but tools

It is my vision, my imagination, and my life's experiences

That gives the picture its life.

Influences

I am influenced by everything and nothing: by my subconscious, the real world, people, colors, songs…

Artists whose work I admire include Matisse, Hockney, Johns, Braque, and Richter. I appreciate their use of color, texture, and space.

RICHARD SWIATLOWSKI

Studio

Software: Painter, Photoshop

Hardware: iMac G5, Wacom Intuos, external HD, HP printer

Contact

Richard Swiatlowski ▪ Spot Photo ▪ Massachusetts, USA ▪ photo.javanet@rcn.com ▪ http://www.art-exchange.com

"On the Boulevard."

Techniques

Step-by-Step Tutorial: "A New York Minute" Photo Collage in Photoshop

I put my images together in Photoshop and then work on them in Painter to intensify the colors and add texture. In this tutorial, I create a simple collage with photographs using Photoshop.

1. Several years ago, I was passing through New York City on a rainy day and used my 35mm film camera to take several photographs from inside my car. Figure 3.1 shows the photograph I have selected as my background image, shot in Times Square. I want to make viewers feel the city's colors and sounds.

Figure 3.1   Select photograph for background image.

2. Now the scene needs a figure and some action, so I select a photograph of a woman taken that same morning. See Figure 3.2.

Figure 3.2   Select elements from other photos.

3. In Photoshop, I use a selection tool to loosely outline the woman and her umbrella. I save the outline as a path and then make the path into a selection. I drag this selection into the Times Square scene, which again is my background. Next, I select one of the Times Square lamppost banners, and I copy and paste it twice onto the other side of the street in front of the tree. See Figure 3.3.

Figure 3.3 Add new elements to the background image.

4. I want to fill the dark billboard in the upper left and balance the image a bit more. I decide to copy and paste a portion of another image into the billboard. See Figure 3.4.

Figure 3.4 Create balance using color.

5. Now the image looks the way I want it to, but the colors are gray and flat. I select Image, Adjustments, Hue/Saturation to brighten the image. I want to see what colors are in there. The yellows come out nicely. See Figure 3.5.

Figure 3.5 Adjust Color Saturation levels.

6. In Figure 3.6, I experiment with Color Balance from the Adjustments menu. I fully increase the Blue setting to find a pleasing complementary color for the yellow taxis.

Figure 3.6 Experiment with Color Balance for contrast.

7. At this point, I am finished in Photoshop. My next steps are to flatten the image and open it in Painter. In Painter, I use the Hard Media Chalk variants to intensify the colors in the yellow cabs, red taillights, and reflections on the street. I also use different paper textures. I paint over the brown car on the right and transform it into another taxi. See Figure 3.7.

Figure 3.7 "A New York Minute," final image.

Step-by-Step Tutorial: Using Paper Textures to Build Up Depth and Richness

I like texture. Even in my traditional media paintings, I build up texture, using layers of paint and scraping, sanding, and scratching until I get the look I want. In Painter, I work a lot with paper textures. I use them to build up colors and depth, which creates an illusion of layers of paint on a flat surface.

While I am working, I use Invert Paper Textures. I adjust Scale and Contrast and change my brushes as well. I change the size of the brush and vary the tip from flat, round, pointed, and so on. When painting, I like to work using the Color Wheel. This way, when I select a shade of blue, paint with it, switch to a red, paint with that, and then select blue again, it isn't exactly the same blue. This creates subtle differences in my image. I also use the Hue, Saturation, and Color Variability sliders to adjust my colors as I paint. I paint a few brushstrokes, change the settings, and paint a few more. I repeat this process, changing paper textures, brush size, media, and colors, building up several layers of paint all over the image. I just play and have fun.

1. At this point, I already have a starting image prepared from my source materials that I have imported and opened in Painter. I begin by selecting my media; I like Pastels/Soft Pastel because it gives me the look of traditional pastels. Under Brush Controls, I pick my settings; Dab is Circular, Stroke is Single, Method is Cover, Subcategory is Grainy Hard Cover, and Expression is Pressure. I change other settings, such as Opacity, Size, and so on, as I work. Next, from the Paper Selector, I select my paper texture; I choose Artists Rough Paper. See Figure 3.8.

Figure 3.8　Import starting image into Painter.

2. I select a color from the Color Wheel and start painting. In Figure 3.9, I add color to the rear of the taxi and to the signboards above using Soft Pastel. As I paint, I continually alter the size of my brushes. I also adjust Paper Scale and Contrast in the Papers palette and keep inverting the paper as I work.

TIP

Inverting the paper texture reverses the tooth of the paper. It is a way to create beautiful color effects and an illusion of depth.

Figure 3.9　Use the Soft Pastel Variant to add color to the image.

3. I continue painting in the same areas with a variety of colors, inverting the paper, changing my brush sizes and colors, and finally building up several layers of paint. After adding color to my satisfaction, I work over every area with the Blenders, Just Add Water brush to blend the colors. I go back and forth with chalk and water until I am satisfied (25 hours). Then I go back into Photoshop and apply a 5 percent contrast to the entire image to unify it. This boosts it a little more and makes the colors pop. See Figure 3.10.

FINE ART

TIP

If you are painting digitally, you really need a drawing tablet!

Figure 3.10   "Another New York Minute: The CATS Billboard," final image.

Insights

The Creative Process

Sometimes I have an idea, but other times I don't. I usually start with photos I have taken. First I open Photoshop and start to put together a collage. I work on composition, colors, and space. Sometimes I include some of my own original artwork. When I am satisfied, I flatten the image and import it into Painter. In Painter, I begin playing with the different brushes and media until I find something that works for the image. I then start painting and making marks. Most of my images take 20 hours in Painter. Once I am satisfied, I take the image back into Photoshop and adjust contrast, saturation, and so on; then I can print it.

Favorite Features

My favorite Painter features are the Paper Textures. I apply Paper Textures to my artwork, changing my choice of papers. I also adjust the Paper Contrast and PaperScale settings for the paper grain while painting, to give a gritty look to my work. Another thing I do as I am painting is use the Invert Paper option because it changes the tooth of the paper. It is a way to create beautiful color-mixing effects that juxtapose varying colors in close proximity by painting into the positive and negative regions of a texture.

Finished Work

It is most important to me that the colors I see on my computer screen are matched as closely as possible in the printing. My finished work is then usually displayed matted and framed under glass.

Q&A

When did you start using Painter?

I started using Painter in the late 1990s.

What do you wish someone had told you when you started?

I wish someone had told me to save my work often! There were several times I had spent hours working on an image when the computer crashed—causing me to lose all the work I had done.

Did you have previous experience in traditional media?

Yes, I had experience in drawing, oil paints, acrylics, pastels, and watercolors.

Do you integrate your work in Painter with traditional artists' materials?

Yes, I do this in two ways. I make a print using archival inks on paper, and then I paint or draw on the print. Other times I take an original painting or drawing and photograph it and then load it into Painter and use digital media to finish.

Has Painter helped you to define your own style?

Yes, being in the digital world, Painter has given me a lot of room to experiment. Also, Painter is where my images really come alive. Most of my time spent working on the images is spent in Painter.

What motivates you?

What motivates me is the thrill of creating. There is nothing as satisfying or as frustrating. Nothing is as vulnerable as my own picture hanging on a wall. I want my pictures to stop you in your tracks and remind you of something.

What advice do you have for artists working with Painter?

Really just get in there and play with all the features Painter has. Try everything until you find your own voice. I still play when I start on a new image. The results can surprise you when you try something different.

Resources

On the DVD

- Artist Gallery

Links

- http://www.mindsisland.com/
- http://www.art.com/gallery/id—a4007/swiatlowski-richard-m-posters.htm
- http://www.apple.com/itunes/
- http://www.hulu.com/

RICHARD SWIATLOWSKI

Education

Self-taught photographic artist

Selected Shows

Alfredo's Photography Gallery, New Jersey Center for Creative Arts, Los Angeles Art Expo, Pivot Gallery, Springfield Museum of Fine Art, Macworld New York, Artworks Gallery

Awards and Career Highlights

Popular Photography Grand Prize
Directors Award Cambridge Art Association

RICHARD SWIATLOWSKI

Gallery

"Madison Square Garden."

"Lions in the Night."

FINE ART

"Cityscape with Statue."

"Smell of Wine & Cheap Perfume."

FINE ART

"Lawyers, Guns, Money."

"The Last Dance."

RICHARD SWIATLOWSKI

FINE ART

"Rue Catherine."

"Hard Luck Bones."

RICHARD SWIATLOWSKI

SONG YANG

About the Artist

I create oil paintings and comics, and my art practice references different styles. I also design, write, and work with video and music. Since I was young, I have shown a talent for drawing, and when I was in college, I had several popular comic works that were published in English, French, and Italian—all in Europe. My work has been exhibited all over China and has won awards in some important comic exhibitions. I have been called both a "vanguard comic artist" as well as a "star-material artist."

I have a column in the magazine *Time Out Beijing* where I interview people from different backgrounds in society and create works of art that are about their lives. These works have been published in media all around the world. I have taken part in the design and creation of work for notorious brands such as Benz, Swarovski, Nike, HUGO BOSS, Tiger Beer, and Yue-Sai. Recently though, I have found my place in contemporary art and have my own style. In 2007, a piece of my work sold for 313,000 RMB! In 2008, I appeared as the youngest judge for the Mascot Designs Collecting Competition at the 26th World University Games. In 2008, I also won the Annual Youth Golden Award for design in Beijing.

Artist's Statement

I use the young, fashionable Chinese style to explain my conception of the world. Through drawing, video, and sculpture, we are able to change our lives.

Influences

I am influenced by love.

SONG YANG

Studio

> Software: Painter, Photoshop

> Hardware: Laptop, Wacom tablet, external drives

Contact

> Song Yang ■ Song Yang Fine Arts Culture Development Co., Ltd. ■ Beijing, China

"Chinese Shanshui Picture and Bad Girl."

Techniques

Step-by-Step Tutorial: Character Painting

1. I select the color background I like and then sketch my character directly in Painter. In Figure 4.1, I use Pencils/2B Pencil.

Figure 4.1 Sketch your character in Painter.

2. I make sure the general color scheme and interrelation of the tones in the painting are consistent. I ask myself questions like, "Is it a classical or modern style?" I have to think it over carefully. See Figure 4.2.

3. I experiment with different Oil Brush variants to start painting. I use them to imitate the Palette Knives effects. In Figure 4.3, I use Image Hose, Linear Variants to add colors that fit within my general color scheme.

Figure 4.2 Choose your style and stay consistent.

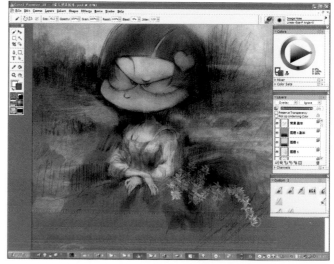

Figure 4.3 Add colors in different layers.

4. I obey the rules for painting: dig deep, adjust my work, and dig deeper. I discover the things I really want. I then add brighter colors in new layers. See Figure 4.4.

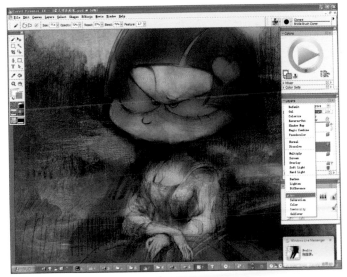

Figure 4.4 Adjust the hue of the colors.

5. There are many special brushes in Painter. I make sure that I am familiar with them and use them properly. In Figure 4.5, I use Artists' Oils, Blender Palette Knife, set at 100 percent Opacity, to add thicker color and texture to the image.

6. I can spend several hours adjusting my painting before I decide it is finished. Because I focus for a long time on my paintings, sometimes it is hard to identify the mistakes. I take a break and come back to make final changes. In Figure 4.6, I have decided that this work is finished now. Figure 4.7 shows the final image.

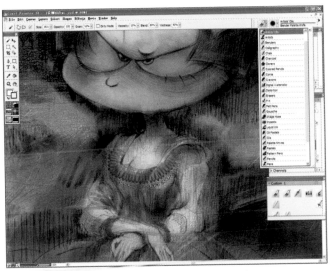

Figure 4.5 Create texture with thick oils.

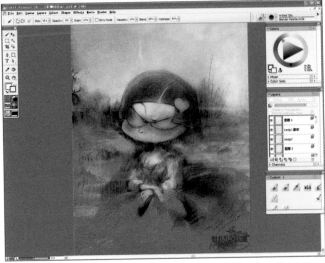

Figure 4.6 Take a break and come back with fresh eyes to finish.

COMIC BOOK ILLUSTRATION

Figure 4.7 "Bad Girl Mona Lisa," final image.

Insights

The Creative Process

I enjoy the process of creating my paintings. I like to sketch directly onto paper or canvas, and I draw using a Wacom tablet in the same way.

Favorite Features

My favorite Painter features are the Mixer Brush and the Oils Brushes. I like the feel of traditional painting strokes.

Customizable Tools

When I want to simulate some old canvas or texture, I adjust the picture with my preset settings. I also have a lab of customized brushes and use them to create small interesting effects, like broken glass, the starlight, and twisting. I use normal strokes to get different effects, both colorful and spiritual!

Finished Work

My finished works are usually displayed as computer graphics, oil paintings, sculpture, or video. The printing quality and design of the work are what is most important to me.

Q&A

When did you start using Painter?

I started using Painter in 2000.

How does Painter fit into your creative process and workflow?

It helps me to upgrade the visual effect of my drawings.

Did you have previous experience in traditional media?
Yes, I have my solo exhibition of oil paintings showing all around the world. This year it is at Galerie Arludik in Paris, France, Gallery Tn in Korea, and 798 in Beijing. I paint on canvas, wood, and various specialty materials.

Do you integrate your work in Painter with other art materials?
Yes, I like to use Photoshop to mix them and to speed up the process for adjusting the color and effects.

Has Painter helped you to define your own style?
Although there are some technical limitations to what computer graphics (CG) can do, especially in extremely large formats, I have learned that Painter, associated with traditional drawing, is the only way to achieve the flawless results I am looking for.

What motivates you?
My friends, my lover, and the things happening all around motivate me. Also, I admire Andy Warhol because he created his own attitude toward art.

How has the Internet influenced your art-making process?
The Internet gives me a chance to see paintings from all around the world. I can know instantly what is happening elsewhere and about changes in the CG area—which gives me the inspiration to mix local culture and fashion to create my own work. Also, I meet a lot of interesting friends through the Internet.

What advice do you have for artists working with Painter?
Try more functions, and you will surprise yourself.

Resources

On the DVD
- Artist Gallery
- Technique Images

Links
- http://www.zhajiang.com
- http://blog.sina.com.cn/songyang

SONG YANG

Education
Graduate of Design College of Tianjin University

Client List
Benz, Swarovski, Nike, HUGO BOSS, Tiger Beer, Yue-Sai

Awards and Career Highlights
2005: 1st Chinese Youth Original Animation and Comic Competition: Best Long Length Comic and Best Art Book awards

2005: Tian Shi Cup Comic and Animation Competition: Promising Youth award

2009: Beijing Youth of Creativity and Design of 2008: Golden award

Selected Shows
2000: Song Yang Personal Comic Exhibition in Urumqi

2004: Exhibitions in Tianjin, Xuzhou, Changzhou, Shanghai, Nanjing, Beijing, and Singapore

2006: *Time Out Beijing* magazine sets up a special column "Song Yang's People" for my drawings

2007–2009: Multiple art and comic exhibitions in China and Europe

2010: Multiple exhibitions worldwide as part of the Bad Girl Music and Art Project

Gallery

"Bad Girl on the Way with the Beatles."

"Fly and Bad Girl."

"Elegance."

"Jena Lee MV."

COMIC BOOK ILLUSTRATION

"Cat."

"Jena Lee MV2 Sky."

COMIC BOOK ILLUSTRATION

"Jena Lee MV Roof."

"The Moon."

SONG YANG

"Girl in Dawn."

既无身体损害，也无危险可言。
只是预订了下周的生活用品，
以及今天的食物。可喜欢比萨
饼么？黏糊糊，甜腻腻，满是
芝士。还有欧式花香酱——具体
是什么也说不好，以前从为试过，
说是充满普罗旺斯的花香来的，
禁不住预订电话的软磨硬泡，
就索性要了一个。

"Servant."

"Couv Reload."

"SongYang Art."

AILEEN STRAUCH

About the Artist

I am a freelance illustrator and comic artist specializing in manga and anime-inspired artwork. I have always had great interest in art and have been an avid fan of manga and anime from a young age. I am originally self-taught but have decided to take my initial hobby further and broaden my skills. I love to tell stories with my illustrations—even if it is just to capture a moment in time. Among other things, my work includes a written tutorial for *ImagineFX* magazine. I have also taught drawing workshops and demonstrated for Wacom. I am currently working with a writer on an online manga project titled "R.P.G."

Artist's Statement

Overall, I simply have fun when I draw. Drawing is something I greatly enjoy, and I can't imagine not being creative in one way or another. I can express emotions with my art, tell stories, or address the viewer directly—and the manga and anime style is my tool of choice to convey just that. It is an aesthetically pleasing form of art, but this does not mean it should only work on the surface. I aim to create pictures that are interesting and keep the attention of the viewer; I want to portray characters who have a history and life behind them.

Influences

I am predominantly producing manga- and anime-inspired art currently, so I mostly look at the Japanese drawing style. However, I do feel it is important to be open minded and to have a general understanding of art. I enjoy art for what it is and for what the creator wants to tell me. I cannot put a finger on what exactly inspires me and influences my work. Quite often music is the trigger for an idea, a theme, or a little story that I can tell with a picture. Looking at other people's art is inspiring in the same way. Picking a manga/anime style to work with does not necessarily restrict me; it is more a tool I like to play with. I guess I have always been intrigued because it is so different from other Western styles.

AILEEN STRAUCH

Studio

Software: Painter, Photoshop

Hardware: Mac, CanoScan 8800F, Wacom Intuos 4

Contact

Aileen Strauch ■ Berlin, Germany ■ leenlet@hotmail.com ■ http://www.kiwichameleon.com

Techniques

Step-by-Step Tutorial: Manga Character Illustration Techniques

In recent years, manga and anime have become increasingly popular, especially with the younger crowd, thus carrying many stereotypes for people who are not familiar with it. Manga is not just big-eyed girls in frilly dresses, and it is not exclusively for kids. Manga and anime come in all forms and sizes, for both young and old. It can be amazingly stylized or very realistic, and there is something suitable for every taste. In general, manga and anime are a line-based art form, in which only a few lines carry expression.

In the following steps, I describe some illustration techniques I use when I am working on a manga illustration: creating volume, styling hair, and creating texture.

For the following step-by-step instructions, I decide to put a single character into focus: a shaman. I use both Photoshop and Painter.

1. To start my illustration, I draw the outlines of my character on paper and scan the image at 300dpi into Photoshop. I adjust the brightness and contrast until I get some crisp lines. I want to work with the pencil lines to achieve a softer look for the final image. To create standalone outlines that I can color, I highlight all the channels and, in the Channels palette, I select Load Channel as Selection. Now only the outlines are selected. See Figure 5.1. I click Delete to get rid of the white background paper.

Figure 5.1 Create image outlines in Photoshop.

> **TIP**
>
> **When working with scanned line art, it is important to clean up the scanned image if needed. Dust or dark particles in the paper can show up in the scanned version.**

2. In Figure 5.2, I deselect the outlines and toggle Preserve Transparency. This allows me to color the lines. Additionally, I create a white background layer so I can see the lines better. I color the outlines black for now, to restore their original line thickness. I save the image as a PSD file to preserve the layers.

> **TIP**
>
> **Always save your work at regular intervals, and name your layers to avoid confusion.**

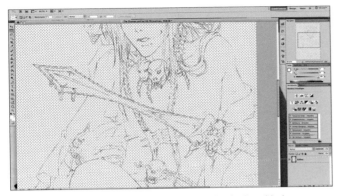

Figure 5.2   Preserve transparency and color lines black.

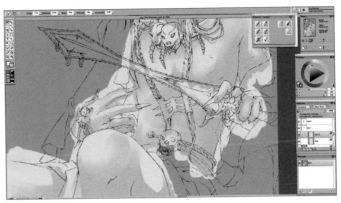

Figure 5.3   Multiply image layers to create volume.

3. I begin to create volume. I import my drawing into Painter
and block in base colors with an Acrylics Brush. For the
shaman, I choose an earthy color scheme with some contrasting highlights since contrasting colors will make the
image more interesting. I start to put down the shadows
roughly, which I then define and add detail to. I build up
color on several layers to create the volume I'm after. Next,
I color the skin: I select a color that contrasts slightly with
either the hair or clothes—whichever is more prominent.
Because I want the cloth to be green, I choose a reddish skin
tone. On top, I paint the first layer with the shadow color.
I set the layer to multiply and use a light red to add the
shadow and define some muscles. With the light red, I want
to bring out the redness of the base skin color. I work with
the Oils, Camelhair Round Brush, but instead of the typical
oil brush profile, I change it to Dab Type, Watercolor Camel
Hair in the General palette. This makes the brushstrokes soft,
yet I still get some color variants when I apply it. It also works
well with the pressure sensitivity of my pen. It is perfect to
blend colors without diluting them. I use Blender, Just Add
Water to soften some edges. See Figure 5.3.

NOTE

Just because this is a manga illustration does not mean it
has to look flat in terms of color and shading. Imagining
the shapes as 3D objects helps to place shadows that
follow a light source. A combination of softly fading shades
and hard shadows adds visual interest.

TIP

To create volume, I mix warm with cold colors, and I often
set the layers to Multiply to get an additive effect.

4. After a further layer of red, I use a grayish purple to tone down the redness in the areas where I need the darker shadows. The technique I use is the same as before. I roughly add the purple shadow and then blend it into the rest of the shadow, leaving it crispier where the cast shadow should be stronger. See Figure 5.4.

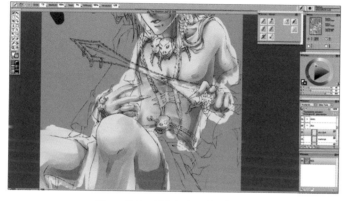

Figure 5.4   Add shadows for depth.

5. In Figure 5.5, to darken some of the shadows, I sparingly use an even darker purple. Occasionally I add green to the dark shadows, which better ties the skin to the green cloth. I also highlight some lighter parts of the skin, such as the cheeks or the knee, by adding a cool light blue with the Airbrush at low opacity. It is barely visible, but it makes the skin more radiant.

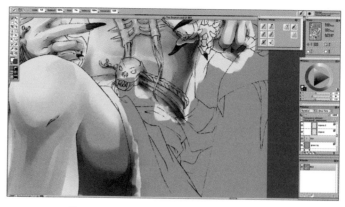

Figure 5.5   Use a variety of colors for skin tones.

6. Next, I style the hair. I decide that I want the shaman's hair color to be black; however, black does not necessarily mean pitch-black. Often black should include some sort of color for shading to avoid flatness. My base color for the hair is a dark warm gray. My choice of base hair color is also important for the shine later on. I add some purple areas because I want the shaman's hair to be two colors. With a small Oils Brush, I work the purple into the hair until it looks "naturally grown." See Figure 5.6.

> **NOTE**
>
> Hair color often represents a character's attributes or personality in anime and manga. It can appear in any color, and some hairstyles even defy gravity, though my personal preference leans toward more realistic hair.

Figure 5.6   Use multiple colors for the hair.

7. I define the hair further with a grayish orange and set the following layers to multiply. I don't use black or neutral gray at all. As I did with the skin, I build up color to the desired effect. In the Japanese style, single hairs are seldom drawn. Instead, hair strands and a few single stray hairs create the illusion. See Figure 5.7.

Figure 5.7   Define sections of hair and build up color.

8. A typical trait of the manga style is to add highlights to the hair. These highlights shouldn't be pure white because that would look too harsh. Color highlights are better suited. I toggle Pick Up Underlying Color in the Layers palette and add bright yellow highlights on a separate layer. This nicely blends the color into the hair. On top, I use the F-X, Glow Brush with a low Opacity setting to create a barely visible glow at the top of the highlight. Finally, I clean up the hair with a sharp-edged eraser. See Figure 5.8.

Figure 5.8   Add highlights to the hair sparingly.

9. I turn my attention to creating texture. Two opposing materials in this picture are the cloth and metal. The shaman wears a heavy cloth, which is why I paint a few folds with big rough brushstrokes while keeping the light source in mind. See Figure 5.9.

> ## NOTE
>
> By texture, I don't mean to include certain textures, but to portray the appearance of different materials. This adds depth and a certain sense of realism to the stylized image.

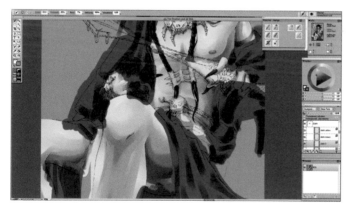

Figure 5.9 Use large strokes to create folds in the fabric.

10. I define the folds further with a smaller brush, and I soften edges to create a gradient effect using a Blender. See Figure 5.10.

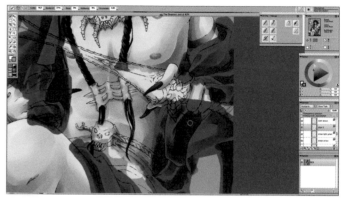

Figure 5.10 Add definition to the folds and soften the edges.

11. I add further dark areas to the shadows with a grayish purple. To enhance the look of the cloth, I paint stripes in several colors on a layer above the base color and underneath the shadows. This makes it easier to let the stripes follow the form and folds of the textile. The Pick Up Underlying Color option comes in handy once again. See Figure 5.11.

Figure 5.11 Add stripes in a separate layer.

12. In Figure 5.12, I paint the horns dull beige as the base color and add shades of dull purple to accentuate the grooved surface. At the same time, the purple picks up the hair's color. On the left horn at the bottom, I apply a touch of green with the Airbrush as a light reflection from the cloth.

Figure 5.12 Texturing the horns.

13. The ceremonial sword is made of both partly polished and matte metals. In contrast to the cloth, I apply mostly sharp brushstrokes with little fading. The key is to leave the strokes angular when portraying this smooth surface. See Figure 5.13.

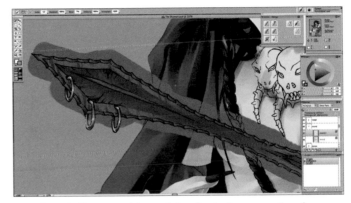

Figure 5.13 Use straight, angled strokes to show a smooth surface.

14. In Figure 5.14, I add small dark details to the reflections and randomly place highlights on the metal sword.

Figure 5.14   Add reflection and highlights to the metal.

16. Now that the character as a whole is finished, I will start work on the background using the same techniques I have described here. Figure 5.16 shows the completed image.

15. Now that the coloring of the character is finished, I adjust some colors with the Color Correction tool. I also color the outlines to get a soft look. See Figure 5.15. It is important to have the Transparency box checked for this.

Figure 5.15   Adjust the color using Color Correction.

Figure 5.16   "The Shaman: Beyond the Invisible."

Insights

The Creative Process

Often I brainstorm ideas when I start on a project, unless I already have something specific in mind. My next step always includes rough sketches to lay down composition and structure. I rarely sketch something without a bit of planning. Once I am satisfied with the rough sketch, I go on to draw a clean sketch where I add details. The steps after this can vary, depending on the overall look I seek. I either trace the outlines, or I work straight into color. When I work with color, I like to work spontaneously. In contrast to the image outlines, I am tempted to break the slight rigidity with lighter brushstrokes.

Favorite Features

My favorite features in Painter include the brushes, which emulate traditional media, and the ability to adjust them to my needs. Also, the custom palettes allow me a place to drop the brushes I use most. This feature is handy and time saving. Finally, being able to rotate the canvas plays a crucial part during my work process and makes working a lot easier.

Customizable Tools

My primary tools are the brushes I use for my artwork. To achieve a painterly look, I change the settings until I get the effect I am looking for. I always use a preset brush as the basis for a new one.

Timesaving Tips

First and foremost, my biggest timesaver is planning—as boring as that might sound. Nothing is worse than having an undefined idea, because it can take up a lot of unnecessary time when you're working toward the finished product. When I use Painter, I often have an idea in my head of what the finished image should look like, which is especially true regarding colors. Creating quick color sketches at the beginning saves me valuable time and prevents me from changing my whole color scheme at the end. Of course, I also love using keyboard shortcuts, such as the mandatory Cmd+Z (Ctrl+Z). Knowing them by heart is invaluable.

> **TIP**
>
> Collect images of the ideas you have for pictures; you never know when you might need them. You can use them to build an archive of reference images.

Finished Work

My finished work is displayed both in print and in digital form. It is important for me to be satisfied with my work and put my best into the pieces I draw. As an artist, I am rarely 100 percent pleased—because I am always striving to get better—but I consider being confident in my work crucial, knowing it is the best I can do at that time.

MANGA ILLUSTRATION

Q&A

When did you start using Painter?
I started to use Painter about three years ago, in 2007.

What do you wish someone had told you when you started?
I wish someone had told me to break out from my traditional approach to creating art, because the change wouldn't have compromised the outcome. I should have been braver, tried different techniques, and experimented with the various brushes instead of sticking to just one kind of brush in the beginning.

Did you have previous experience in traditional media?
I come from a traditional art background and only ventured into digital painting a few years ago. Working traditionally has always been fulfilling for me, but I would not want to miss working digitally these days. Apart from the typical pencil, fine liner, and brush pen, I enjoy working with markers, although I am not sure if this medium can be called traditional per se. Occasionally I work with watercolors, too.

Do you integrate your work in Painter with traditional artists' materials?
When I am working with Painter, I like to keep most of my image digital, with the exception of my first step in creating an image: the sketch. I am a big fan of drawing my sketches on paper rather than on the computer. I scan my outlines and continue work from there.

Has Painter helped you define your own style?
Ever since I started to draw digitally, I have wanted to achieve an organic look. I want to create a painterly style with my coloring, not a clinical cleanliness. I find that I can achieve this in Painter. Painter lets me work freely, and the traditional elements of the program really do appeal to me.

How does Painter fit into your creative process and workflow?
Painter gives me the means to be creative and offers me security in what I want to portray. I can work from an idea toward a desired result, and I always have the option to change my image if I feel I need to. Painter helps me when I want to try out new ideas, especially when I test new effects or techniques.

What motivates you?
Ever since I was little, I have enjoyed being creative, and drawing in particular. Drawing is something I cannot live without. It is relaxing as well as challenging, and I always want to learn new things. The constant attempt to improve my artwork is a huge driving force for me. It is important to set new goals for myself.

Which artists do you admire?
I hope this is not a weird answer, but I have to say no one in particular—there are so many artists out there, past and present, whose work I admire. Sometimes it is just a single piece that strikes me, a certain technique, or even a message. I find it interesting to see and compare what people produced hundreds of years ago to what people are painting today, but I still feel unable to pin down a few specific artists.

How has the Internet influenced your art-making process?
The Internet is such a vast space that it is nearly impossible to say it has not influenced my art and how I work. When I am looking for references, if I want to browse art, or when I want to look up some information, the Internet is easy to access, and I can literally find anything I am looking for. Without the Internet, I am not sure where I would be with my art today. In hindsight, it is because of the Internet and the art I have seen via this medium that I picked up digital painting in the first place.

What advice do you have for artists working with Painter?

I would say get to know the Painter program and what it is capable of. Try out the functions. Play with the brushes. Experiment. Sometimes I find new brushes to use for my images that I have not thought about using before. Painter is about the process of painting, not fancy filters. I like to treat it more like a traditional tool instead of something overly digital. I don't want the program to do the work for me; I want to do it myself. Painter is perfect for emulating traditional art media with a digital advantage.

Since I started using Painter, it has occurred to me that this software is not as widely used for manga and anime illustrations as I thought it would be. Painter is a great tool for people who have a traditional art background—which is often true of fans of manga and anime-inspired artwork.

Resources

On the DVD

- Artist Gallery

Links

- http://www.kiwichameleon.com
- http://www.imaginefx.com
- http://www.conceptart.org
- http://www.deviantart.com
- http://www.posemaniacs.com/blog
- http://www.tokyoluv.com
- http://www.sweatdrop.com
- http://rpgmanga.com
- http://en.wikipedia.org/wiki/Manga
- http://en.wikipedia.org/wiki/Anime
- http://en.wikipedia.org/wiki/Lolita_fashion

AILEEN STRAUCH

Education

BA (honors) film: video production with film studies, Thames Valley University, London
Manga drawing and coloring workshops and demonstrations

Client List

Japanese Art Festival (London); AmeCon; Wacom (UK); Cultbranding.com; ImagineFX; *Neo* magazine; *Disorder* magazine

Awards and Career Highlights

R.P.G. online manga

Gallery

"I've Got Something for You!"

"Dark Cherry."

MANGA ILLUSTRATION

"Yummy Pink."

"MJ."

"Reflection."

WONMAN KIM

About the Artist

I am a self-taught illustrator and conceptual designer who has been working in this career for 10 years. In past years, I worked as an environment and character concept designer for several game development companies. I have also illustrated children's and adult books. Recently, I started making graphic T-shirt and toy designs. I love painting subjects with fantasy and science fiction themes.

Artist's Statement

I hope to please everybody who sees my illustrations. Illustration is a tool to open the window of an artist's mind.

Influences

Movies, animation, games, and professional artists' paintings are all inspiring to me. I especially admire the illustrations of Leyendecker, N. C. Wyeth, and talented computer graphics (CG) artists like Craig Mullins, Jaime Jones, Kekai Kotaki, Justin Sweet, Jon Foster, Khang Le, and Tomer Hanuka. I find Craig Mullins to be an extremely inspiring artist; his matte paintings and games-promo artwork are awesome. He is currently the leading CG artist in the industry today.

WONMAN KIM

Studio

Software: Painter, Photoshop, particleIllusion

Hardware: IBM Intel Core 2 Duo CPU E7500

Contact

Wonman Kim ▪ Bucheon, South Korea ▪ pimcoo@naver.com
http://www.abart.co.kr

"Setout."

Techniques

Step-by-Step Tutorial: "Samurai War"

I have decided to illustrate a fight between a group of human Samurai and a Samurai monster. I am using Painter 11, Photoshop CS3, and particleIllusion for this process.

1. I begin by drawing a rough sketch. Usually, I like rough drawings when I start to paint something—sometimes a rough sketch can be more beautiful than a refined image. In Figure 6.1, I sketch roughly with Painter's Oil Pastels, Chunky Oil Pastel 10. I draw a dynamic Samurai monster and some human Samurai figures.

Figure 6.1 Rough sketch with Chunky Oil Pastel.

2. After I sketch in some rough figures and a background, I add some color to the image. I tend to use either Overlay, Hard Light, or Composite method (Default) to add color to my paintings. See Figure 6.2.

Figure 6.2 Adding color to the rough sketch.

3. In Figure 6.3, I begin to refine my rough sketch. I change the Samurai monster's weapon and refine the armor. I like to keep the design flexible, and I usually change it frequently.

4. In Figure 6.4, I decide to change the colors in the atmosphere from brown to green and move the castle in the background from right to left. I also decide to add light from flames to the foreground in front of the figures. This means that the light from the flames will affect everything located in front.

Figure 6.3 Begin to refine the rough sketch.

Figure 6.4 Change the color and add light from flames.

WONMAN KIM

93

5. I create a new layer to paint the flames' light. I use Acrylics, Captured Bristle and make sure to check Pick Up Underlying Color. If I don't check this box, my new layer won't recognize the colors in the bottom layer. See Figure 6.5.

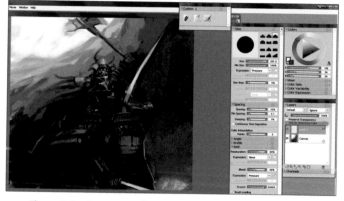

Figure 6.5   Create a new layer and select Pick Up Underlying Color.

6. In Figure 6.6, I add a new figure to the foreground. I also decide to delete the castle from the background. At this stage in my painting, I want the focus to be mainly on the figures.

Figure 6.6   Add another figure and simplify the background.

7. Next, I try rotating the Canvas layer a bit. I decide to do this because I think a slightly twisted angle will make the sword fight seem more dramatic. See Figure 6.7.

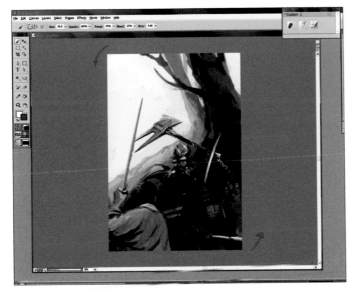

Figure 6.7 Rotate the canvas slightly.

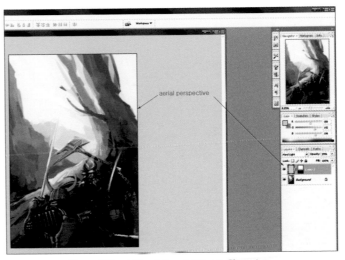

Figure 6.8 Add aerial perspective in Photoshop.

8. Now I want to add aerial perspective, so I import my image into Photoshop. In Photoshop, I add a light blue color in a new layer using Hard Light. See Figure 6.8. For this, I reduce the opacity and add a layer mask. This brings an aerial perspective effect to my painting.

9. In this next step, I take my image back into Painter and decide that it's time to refine the shapes and colors some more. I use Digital Watercolor, Simple Water to do this. For Method, I select Cover instead of Wet. See Figure 6.9. I also add a bright color to the armor on the figures to show backlighting from the light of the flames. See Figure 6.10.

Figure 6.9 Refine shapes and colors.

Figure 6.10 Add light from the flames to the armor.

10. At this time, I stop to note the distance of each object in the image. Figure 6.11 shows the different areas that I pay attention to. I want to express appropriate lights and shadows for each object according to its distance.

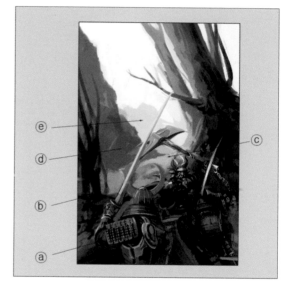

Figure 6.11 Highlight according to distance.

11. Using personal photographs taken from nature, I add some texture throughout the whole image. The textures enrich and add depth to the illustration. I am careful to add texture only slightly, not excessively. See Figure 6.12.

12. I continue to refine and add details to all the Samurai. See Figure 6.13.

Figure 6.12   Add texture to the illustration.

Figure 6.13   Close-up: refining the artwork step by step.

13. Using Oil Pastels and Acrylics as my brushes, I freely work on the background. I adjust the value of each brush's spacing options so that each brush makes its stroke unique and gives the effect of an oil painting. See Figure 6.14.

Figure 6.14   Paint the background with Acrylics and Oil Pastels.

14. Next, I take my image back into Photoshop. I use a custom brush that I have made there. I select Scattering as an option and adjust the Angle Jitter. I usually use this brush when I make trees and leaves. See Figure 6.15.

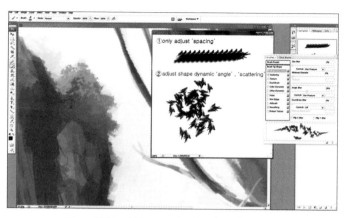

Figure 6.15   Add custom brushwork in Photoshop.

15. Referring back to the areas I noted in step 10 Figure 6.11, I refine areas A and E using different brushes for each. I add light in front of the tree (area C) to give a feeling of distance. See Figure 6.16. I select Linear Light in a new layer to make the lighting on the side of the tree and on the grass and bushes. See Figure 6.17. I think this illustration is about 70 percent complete now!

16. Taking my image back into Painter now, in Layers, I select Multiply and make the shading even deeper. I want the figures in front to stand out more obviously than the other Samurai. See Figure 6.18.

Figure 6.16   Use different brushes to refine individual areas.

Figure 6.17   Select Linear Light in Photoshop.

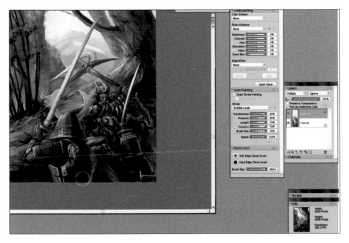

Figure 6.18 Deepen shadows on the front figures.

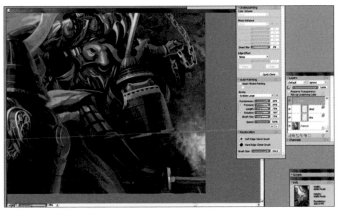

Figure 6.20 Fire effect added to the image in Painter.

17. Next, I create a fire effect using particleIllusion software (see Figure 6.19) and add it to my image. I make sure to check out its alpha value. See Figure 6.20.

18. In Figure 6.21, I add more color to the atmosphere. To make the scene seem more dramatic, I decide that I want it to look like it's taking place at dusk rather than in broad daylight. I adjust the Hue Value and add blue light to the entire image. I also create a glow effect on the edges of the Samurai swords and on the armor. To do this, I use the F-X, Glow Brush. See Figure 6.22.

19. I am almost done with this illustration, so I open Photoshop and import my image. I adjust Hue/Saturation, Color Balance, and Levels. See Figure 6.23.

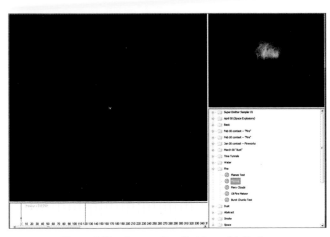

Figure 6.19 Create a fire effect in particleIllusion.

CONCEPT ART/ILLUSTRATION

Figure 6.21 Change the atmosphere of the scene.

Figure 6.23 Adjust Hue and Color Balance in Photoshop.

Figure 6.22 Use the F-X, Glow Brush to add highlights.

20. Back in Painter again, I add more side lighting at the base of the tree. To do this, I first make a duplicate layer and use the Apply Lighting option. I use this to make light look like it's coming subtly from above and the side. I slightly adjust each value of brightness, distance, spread, exposure, and light color. I like the way the lighting seems more fantastic now. See Figure 6.24.

TIP

Using the Apply Lighting effect can save a lot of time when rendering, but be careful; too much light effect can make your work look flat.

21. To finish my illustration, I want to create some "flame flakes" that will give the effect of fire flaming quickly in front of a camera. I paint the flakes by selecting Charcoal, Gritty Charcoal and adjusting the Angle, Spacing, and Size options with Expression set to Pressure. See Figure 6.25.

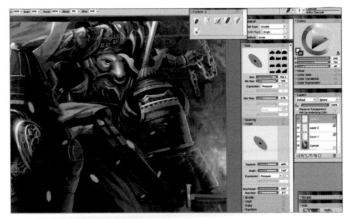

Figure 6.25   Create flakes of fire and soften the edges.

22. Next, I select some flakes and soften them. I go to Effects, Focus, Soften, and then select Gaussian as the aperture. I also use Effects, Focus, Motion Blur. This gives me the effect I am looking for, and I decide that I am finished with "Samurai War." See Figure 6.26.

Figure 6.24   Use Apply Lighting to add natural directional lighting.

Figure 6.26 "Samurai War," final image.

Insights

The Creative Process

I have no specific creative process. In most cases, my work process is rough but flexible. When I start a new piece, I have a vague idea of what I want to paint, but most of my ideas actually develop while I'm painting. I work with Painter and Photoshop and switch often between the two.

Favorite Features

I love Painter's Watercolor Brushes because they are variable and creative. The Digital Watercolor details on the property bar, such as Diffusion and Wet Fringe, are awesome. Sometimes I work using a wet-on-dry technique by painting wet, dry, wet, dry, wet, dry, and so on. Using the Watercolor Brushes is sometimes difficult and complicated, but it's also interesting.

Customizable Tools

I collect and customize my favorite brush tools, including the Oil Pastels, Acrylics, Digital Watercolor, and the F-X, Glow Brush.

Finished Work

My artwork is usually published in a book. The most important thing that I consider when finishing my work is its initial intention and concept.

Q&A

When did you start using Painter?

I started using Painter approximately 10 years ago.

What do you wish someone had told you when you started?

Painter is a god. Ha ha!

Did you have previous experience in traditional media?

I learned acrylic painting a few years ago.

Has Painter helped you to define your own style?

Maybe. Painter creates my artwork and allows it to flourish deeply.

How does Painter fit into your creative process and workflow?

Using Painter makes my digital art look a lot more like traditionally painted artwork. This is great. Having the Wetness control is really cool.

Do you integrate your work in Painter with traditional artists' materials?

I hope to integrate traditional art into my work, but it is difficult. I hope to integrate John Singer Sargent's brush technique.

How has the Internet influenced your art-making process?

The Internet is an excellent resource for finding and collecting good image references.

What advice do you have for artists working with Painter?

Find differences and similarities between traditional media and Painter, and learn to work with them.

Resources

On the DVD

- Artist Gallery

Links

- http://www.abart.co.kr
- http://forums.cgsociety.org/
- http://cghub.com
- http://gurneyjourney.blogspot.com/
- http://www.wondertouch.com/pIllusion3.asp
- http://www.conceptart.org

WONMAN KIM

Education

Self-taught animator, gaming concept designer, and freelance illustrator

Client List

KRGsoft; Nexon; Hangame; Korea Piaget; Little Land; Itempool; Sisongsa; Hemingway, Woongjin Thinkbig; Uneetee; Ballistic

WONMAN KIM

CONCEPT ART/ILLUSTRATION

Gallery

"Aviation."

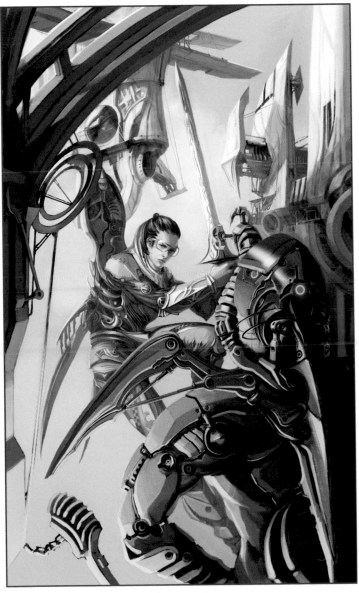

"Encounter."

CONCEPT ART/ILLUSTRATION

"Biker Krampus."

"Catacomb."

"Dragon Hunter."

"Gunman."

BRIAN HABERLIN

About the Artist

I am an artist and writer working in most entertainment media from film to comics. I am known as an innovator and creator of most of the modern production and computer art methods used in the comic industry today. I have created many comic book properties, including Stone, Aria, Hellcop, and Area 52. I write for *3dWorld Magazine*, and I teach at Minneapolis College of Art and Design and my own online company: DigitalArtTutorials.com. For another company of mine, Anomaly Productions, I am currently creating new graphic novels that will be coming out in 2011.

Artist's Statement

I have an "everything but the kitchen sink" approach. I believe in being an all-rounder—able to paint in oils one day, sculpt digitally the next, write and create later the same day, and then fuse all these skills into one product. Illustration and sequential storytelling are that ticket for me. I have always felt that a pretty picture deserves a good story to go along with it.

Influences

Great artists, both fine and commercial, influence me. Let me break it down for who does what really well: for dynamic action, I admire the work of Marko Djurdjevic; for expressively rendered figures, Egon Schiele; for design, Gustav Klimt; for awesome painting, Phil Hale; for simplicity in story-telling and design, Moebius (Jean Henri Gaston Giraud). Really, my list could go on and on as I look around at the books in my studio. It really depends on who I've been looking at lately—so it is fluid and changes. Great directors like Peter Jackson, David Fincher, and Alfred Hitchcock, and great shows and movies, from *Lost* to *Seven*, also influence me.

BRIAN HABERLIN

Studio

Software: Painter, Photoshop, Poser

Hardware: i7-980x PC, Wacom Cintiq

Contact

Brian Haberlin ■ California, USA ■
http://www.digitalarttutorials.com

"First Page from Anomaly Graphic Novel."

Techniques

Step-by-Step Tutorial: Create a Pattern Brush... "The Spawn Way!"

I was lucky enough to draw Todd McFarlane's comic *Spawn* for a couple of years before moving on to my own creations. I learned a lot—especially about timesaving techniques. A comic is 22 pages, plus a cover, every month, so it's a lot of work. One of Spawn's powers is the animated chains he uses to…well, kick ass! I have a fairly detailed and realistic pen-and-ink style, so doing hundreds of chains would take me a long time! My solution was to create a Chain Pattern Pen that would allow me to freely draw hundreds of chains in mere seconds. Here's how:

1. Acquire a chain; it can be a photo, a drawing, or even a 3D model. For this example, I use a 3D digital model: I use Poser software to render a length of chain and save it as a PNG file. See Figure 7.1.

Figure 7.1   Rendered chain sample.

2. In Figure 7.2, I import and open the image in Painter. I select the layer with the chain to be the active layer. Because this is a PNG file, the chain is already nicely masked off.

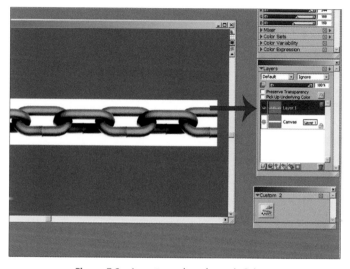

Figure 7.2   Import sample and open in Painter.

> ## NOTE
>
> If I were using a different image file type, I would have to select the part that I want to be the pattern. Also, if I choose an image with a white background, it will not be transparent when drawing, and it will not look correct.

3. With the image selected, I go to the Patterns palette menu and select Capture Pattern. See Figure 7.3. I choose a name for my new pattern. I usually find that the default settings of Rectangular Tile and Bias at 0 percent work well. I click OK.

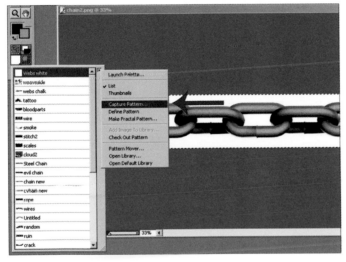

Figure 7.3 Select Capture Pattern.

4. In my Pattern Selector, I can see my new pattern. See Figure 7.4. It's time for me to take it for a spin. I select Pattern Pens from the Brush Category, and under Brush Variant, I select Pattern Pen.

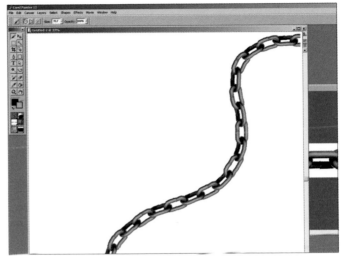

Figure 7.4 My new pattern.

5. Now I draw! I see a chain that wraps with my strokes. I decide to change it so that it appears to work in perspective. Under the Brush Control palette (Window, Brush Controls), in the Size menu, I choose both the size (Size) and the minimum size (Min. Size) of my brush. This way, by using pen pressure as my tool for expression, I can draw the chains larger and smaller in space to make my image appear more three dimensional. See Figure 7.5.

TIP

Try using your pattern as a painting tool by selecting Brush Variant, Pattern Chalk. You can really create some unique images.

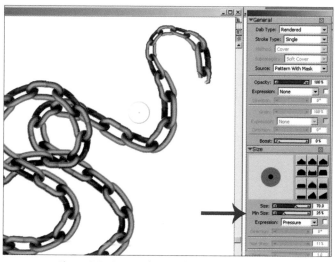

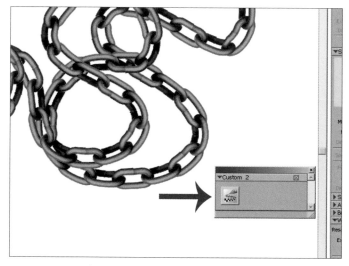

Figure 7.5 Use Brush Control to create perspective.

Figure 7.6 Create a Custom Brush palette.

6. I click and drag my new Pattern Brush from the Brush Selector menu. This creates a new palette with my Custom Pattern Brush—now at my fingertips' convenience for future use. See Figure 7.6.

7. After looking at the brush pattern, I decide I need to take it one step further. After all, because this is chain for Spawn, it could be a bit more evil looking. With my original chain pattern opened (the PNG file), I select Brush Category, Distortion and Brush Variant, Distorto. Now it's easy for me to pull out spikes on my chain. See Figure 7.7. I follow my earlier steps to save this as a custom spiky-chain brush.

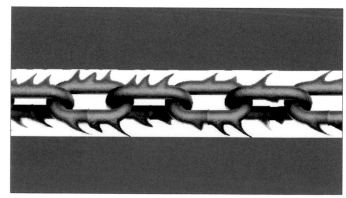

Figure 7.7 Using Distortion, Distorto to create spikes on the chain.

8. I use this same technique for wires, Spiderman's webs, rope, and fabric design—and, of course, all of Spawn's chains. The applications really are unlimited! You can see how I use my custom chain pattern in a drawing in Figure 7.8.

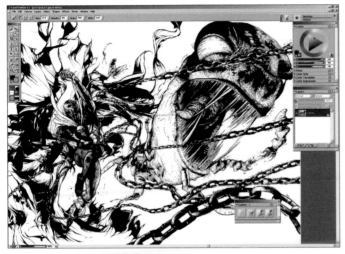

Figure 7.8 Use of chain pattern in a drawing—final image.

TIP

Draw a sketch mark, make it into a **Custom Pattern Brush**, and then draw something with it—your marks will be unique. It's almost like creating an entirely new drawing tool.

Step-by-Step Tutorial: Creating Natural Pattern Pens

The key to a unique painting is the type of marks made on the canvas. I use Pattern Pens to create natural looks—perhaps even more realistic than Painter's own built-in brushes. With the following technique, you will have a method for creating all types of marks and making them your own.

1. I start by making two pages of marks using traditional watercolor paints on paper, and then I scan them onto my computer. I save them in PSD format. In Figure 7.9, I open them both in Painter.

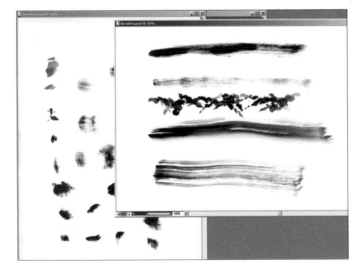

Figure 7.9 Use traditional art tools to make marks on paper.

2. I decide to capture these brushes a bit differently from my chain pattern because I will be using them as brushes to paint with. I use the Rectangular Selection tool to select around one of my brush shapes. There is no need to use layers. See Figure 7.10.

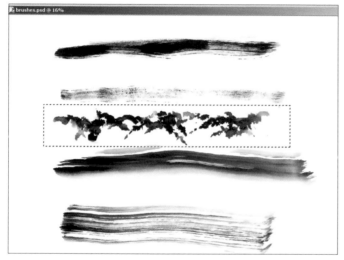

Figure 7.10   Use the Rectangular Selection tool to capture the marks individually.

3. Now I follow the same steps as outlined in the preceding technique, "Create a Pattern Brush," to capture and name my pattern. See Figure 7.11.

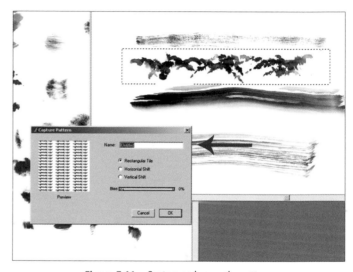

Figure 7.11   Capture and name the pattern.

NOTE

You can design long texture brushes in Painter that curve convincingly, as opposed to in Photoshop, where the stroke doesn't curve as well and ends up looking like rectangles of the image you used to make the brush.

4. Figure 7.12 shows a sampling of four of my brushstrokes. I apply them with the Pattern Pens, Pattern Pen Masked Brush. I am able to pick any colors I like to draw with, and the marks look really natural. I use them to add an even more natural feel to my paintings by either adding them throughout my working process or touching up a painting with them.

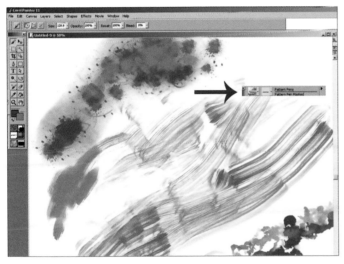

Figure 7.12 Select any color and make traditional-looking marks— final image.

Insights

The Creative Process

Ideas come as they please—either as just a pop, or as hearing or seeing something and twisting it. I play the "what if" game, so to speak. From there, it's on to the sketch pad. I use plain old paper and some type of drawing implement, and I start designing. I draw different versions of what my idea is, or if it's a story, I start to break out the elements and characters. Ideas keep popping into my head, and I have to express them one way or the other. I think if I didn't, my brain would just pop.

Favorite Features

I like the way I can make brushes with full textures and colors. I use these to create things that would be time consuming to draw every time. For example, when I was drawing Spawn, he had these chains that would emanate from him, and he'd fight with them. Drawing every link, over and over, would be a pain, but with Painter, I just created a section and made it into a Pattern Brush. Now I just draw wherever I want the chains to go in a scene.

Customizable Tools

You simply *have* to make a custom tool palette, because there are too many choices in Painter. Most artists get lost trying them all. I recommend grabbing your favorite tools, tweaked or not, and putting them into a custom palette. You'll stay much saner that way.

BRIAN HABERLIN

TIP

To get a handle on creating your own patterns, go to Window, Library Palettes, Patterns. This opens the Patterns palette. On the Patterns palette, go to Pattern Selector. On the side drop-down menu, select Check Out Pattern. This shows the original pattern used to create the brush and allows editing.

Timesaving Tips

Before jumping into any program—from 3D to paint—I recommend a battle plan. A thumbnail, or multiple thumbnails, can serve as a road map to your creation. Most digital tools are so limitless in their abilities that you can easily drain time away by using a program without a clear plan. A small thumbnail sketch, no more than a couple of inches, will give you that road map and not stifle your creative flow on the computer by being too tight.

Finished Work

My artwork is usually seen in print, so it is normally reproduced as large Epson prints on nice matte- or watercolor-type papers. I consider accurate color reproduction to be the most important thing to consider when publishing my finished work. I can spend forever working on a piece, but if I don't have control over the way it is finally reproduced, it can be all for naught.

Q&A

When did you start using Painter?
My first Painter "can" was Painter 1.

Did you have previous experience in traditional media?
Yes—pretty much everything from watercolor to encaustic. I'm a bit of a mad scientist when it comes to art and really like to explore them all and mix them in ways they are not necessarily supposed to mix.

Do you integrate your work in Painter with traditional artists' materials?
I tend to work in and out of the computer quite often. There is a painting I did that started as a pencil sketch, which I then scanned and painted on in Painter. Next, I printed it onto some nice Canson paper and worked on it some more with Prismacolor pencils, pastels, and gouache.

Has Painter helped you define your own style?
Sometimes style is all about the mark you put upon the canvas. With Painter, I can put down marks that are hard to emulate with other programs.

How does Painter fit into your creative process and workflow?
It really depends on the style of the project I am working on. I prefer sketching in Painter to sketching in Photoshop, and I prefer Painter when painting in a sort of digital-oils style. Like most artists, I use Painter in conjunction with Photoshop on most projects—sometimes I use more Painter than Photoshop, and sometimes it is the other way around.

How has the Internet influenced your art-making process?
Getting reference materials is now a breeze. I just Google (insert what is needed here), and bingo-bango, the old trips to libraries or used book stores are over. Now I just go to libraries and used book stores for fun.

What advice do you have for artists working with Painter?
Take some time. Explore all of Painter's brushes, pick the 5 to 10 that you will use most often, and then create your own custom palette. It's a big timesaver.

Resources

On the DVD
- Artist Gallery
- Support Files

Links
- http://www.digitalarttutorials.com
- http://www.anomalyproductions.com

BRIAN HABERLIN

Education
30 years as a professional artist

Client List
DreamWorks, Disney, Marvel Comics, DC Comics, Adobe Inc., TV Guide, Top Cow Productions, Universal Studios, Warner Bros., *Spin Magazine*, Bandai, Pacific Data Images, Stan Winston Creatures, Sammy Studios, Sprint, NASCAR, and many, many more

Awards and Career Highlights
Wizard Fan Awards—winner of multiple awards; Eisner Award (for studio and part of team); multiple inclusions in Spectrum: *The Best in Contemporary Fantastic Art*; artwork added to the permanent collection of The Smithsonian

COMIC BOOK ILLUSTRATION

Gallery

"Page from Anomaly Graphic Novel."

"Page from Anomaly Graphic Novel."

"Page from Anomaly Graphic Novel."

"AODH."

"Cover to Spawn Comic, Issue 184."

"Inside Cover from Anomaly Graphic Novel."

"Spread from Anomaly Graphic Novel."

BENJAMIN

About the Artist

I am one of the earliest comic artists in China to use a computer and full-color pictures to draw comic stories. Now I am considered by many to be a pioneer of computer graphics (CG) in my country. I create contemporary Chinese comics and illustrations, and my realistic painting style has influenced many other Chinese artists. In China, my novels have met with even more success than my comics. I have created a large number of works about the real life of the Chinese people—avant-garde, and rich in spiritual care and social criticism.

In China, I not only publish comics, novels, magazines, and illustrations, but have founded a school in Beijing to have a positive impact on young people and bring caring and critical thinking into Chinese pop culture.

Artist's Statement

I am the kind of person who is not easily satisfied with himself. As a result, I have tried many different artistic styles. During the 10 years of my career, I've been swinging between different methods: between comic books and novels, between comic books and illustration, between contemporary art and comic books. I have written novels, drawn comics, and painted illustrations. But I was unsure of which style I preferred until recently, when I cleared up my thoughts.

What I like is society and the relationships between people. I like to observe the tangled love, the kinship, the friendship, the desire, the dreams. Then I create stories to reflect the things I

have seen—whether through pictures or words. I have much more passion for paying attention to others and to the community than I do for considering the individual. I spend a lot of time at home drawing, which helps to makes me an even shyer person than I was in the past.

Influences

Almost everyone in my life has brought me inspiration. People can be so funny—sometimes even absurd. For example, I have a friend who is serious by nature, but after getting drunk, he starts climbing trees. Another friend was poor when he was young, but when he became rich, he bought the most expensive car and a telephone made of gold. These things make me laugh. And they all become inspiration for my work.

BENJAMIN

Studio
Software: Painter

Hardware: Wacom Cintiq 21

Contact
Benjamin ■ True Colour International Visual Art College (Hong Kong) Group ■ Beijing, China ■ benben0000@hotmail.com ■ http://blog.sina.com.cn/benjamin

"Then the Last Light of Sun Disappeared—Nightfall."

Techniques

Step-by-Step Tutorial: The Creation Process of an Image

1. I want to draw the feeling of a lonely girl who is standing by traffic. She is raising one hand to cover the glaring and overwhelming lights. At the beginning, I use green and blue to make a general composition, because these two colors give me the feeling of loneliness. See Figure 8.1.

Figure 8.1   Create a general composition.

2. During the process, I continue changing the composition. Sometimes it feels like a totally different picture. My process of modifying the composition is crazy; I use the biggest brush and keep covering and modifying the image. I also change the size of the canvas many times; sometimes I make it longer, and sometimes I crop part of it. It's the same for the color; I add color, trying to match different colors, and keep modifying the image. See Figure 8.2.

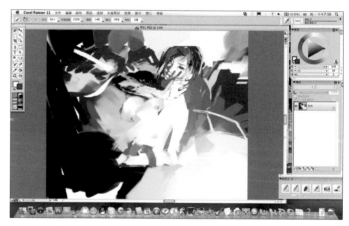

Figure 8.2   Use large brushstrokes to cover the canvas.

3. In Figure 8.3, I make the canvas bigger and decide to add more to the background to highlight the loneliness of the girl. I also consider the whole picture from a different point of view—from that of a person who is in a car looking out.

4. I continue tuning the whole color system of my drawing. Now I make it much more purple. At the same time, I find myself thinking it is not enough for the girl to just raise one hand, so in Figure 8.4, I draw her with two hands raised. The drawing gives a stronger feeling of terror this way.

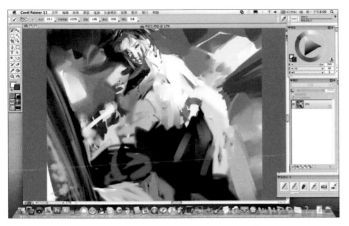

Figure 8.3 Change canvas size and point of view.

Figure 8.4 Experiment with color and composition.

5. I continue to focus on the composition of the image and the action of the girl. I make her expression much clearer and add details. But now I decide that she should have one arm down, with an intention to protect her bag. I also enlarge the canvas further. See Figure 8.5.

Figure 8.5 Begin to focus on facial expression and details.

6. Next, I decide that red and purple are too warm for the emotions in this image, so in Figure 8.6, I use several big brushes to make the picture blue and purple. I also reject my previous action and repaint her with two arms raised.

Figure 8.6 Add new colors to create emotion.

7. Focusing on the background, I decide that I need a less intense blank space. See Figure 8.7.

8. Because a drawing reflects reality, I decide I need an explanation for the blank. I use harsh car lights as my explanation and begin to dig deeper into the background details. I decide to flip the image at this point. I add cars to the street behind the girl and a tall building in the background. During this process, I pay a lot of attention to keeping the drawing cohesive through the use of texture and line. In Figure 8.8, the car lights draw the viewer's focus onto the figure.

Figure 8.7 Keeping the figure as the focal point.

Figure 8.8 Use texture and line to enhance the composition.

9. I continue to add more details. At this point, the most difficult part is to keep the picture whole—to not let too many details eat up the important part of the drawing. Now when either adding or deleting a light, I need to ponder carefully. In Figure 8.9, I add details to the girl's hands and continue to make her expression clearer.

Figure 8.10　Flipping the image.

Figure 8.9　Add details to the most important parts of the image.

10. I make sure to rotate the image occasionally to check for mistakes. This time I decide to leave it this way. See Figure 8.10.

TIP

When I use Painter, I often flip the image I am working on to see if it looks right. Sometimes, without noticing how it happens, the face of the figure I am drawing may look crooked. By flipping the image upside down, my mistakes appear—it is like checking my drawing from a stranger's point of view.

11. My last job here is to soften the sharp and rough edges of the brushstrokes I created during the frenzy of my painting process. I don't want them to become disruptive when I view the finished image. See Figure 8.11.

Figure 8.11   Soften the painted edges.

12. Finished! See Figure 8.12.

Figure 8.12   "Dark Foreboding" final image.

Insights

The Creative Process

Because many of my works are comic stories, I first make a word script out of my thoughts and then begin using Painter to draw. It takes me a lot of time to change the composition of the picture and draw new drafts. During the whole coloring process, I go on pursuing the perfect composition. I do this entire process using only my computer as a tool.

Favorite Features

I usually use a hard brush to draw the main body of the picture. Oil Pastels is one example, because it gives a rough and wild feeling. See Figure 8.13.

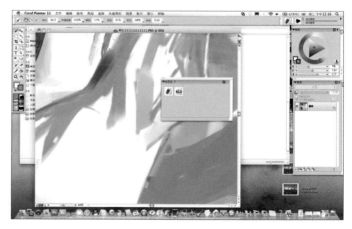

Figure 8.13   Using Oil Pastels to create a spontaneous feeling.

COMIC BOOK ILLUSTRATION

Then, after that, in Figure 8.14, I use Photo, Scratch Remover to melt the edges of the rough brushstrokes. It gives me a subtle transition of color and helps to realize the contrast between the transparent and heavily colored areas.

Figure 8.14　Using Scratch Remover to soften the edges.

Timesaving Tips

To help with switching brushes quickly, I drop all the brushes I like onto one panel. I simply drag and drop the brushes I need onto my work space and use them. See Figure 8.15.

Figure 8.15　Create a palette of favorite brushes and set them onto the workspace.

I can then create a custom toolbox of my most-used brushes and use them much more efficiently. See Figure 8.16.

TIP

Because I change my brushes a lot, I press Ctrl+Alt on my Mac keyboard and then press my Wacom pen onto the tablet screen. This lets me directly change the size of the brush. I find Painter to be much more convenient, faster, and intuitive than Photoshop.

COMIC BOOK ILLUSTRATION

Figure 8.16 Save favorite brushes in a custom palette.

Finished Work

Most of the time, my finished work is printed in comic books. Because I am also a novelist, I sometimes draw the covers and illustrations for my own novels. The color rendering of my printed images is the most important thing I consider when publishing my finished work.

Q&A

When did you start using Painter?

I started using Painter in 1999.

Did you have previous experience in traditional media?

Yes, I did. Many years ago, I devoted myself to drawing on paper, copying the black-and-white style of Japanese manga. After I began using the computer to draw, I almost gave up all the paper-related drawings. Later I created few black-and-white drawings, and then I became an artist playing with colors. Now I am trying watercolor and oil painting.

How has it been for you to learn about using art tools in a digital setting?

Some years ago I quit my job, went to Tianjing to draw comic books, and saved money to buy a computer (which was extremely expensive). I had to go to Beijing to buy a Wacom tablet, because there weren't any in Tianjing. I used the computer to draw for one year. No one taught me how to draw, not even books. I was ignorant—it cost me one year to become familiar with software like Photoshop, and then Painter. But once I became familiar with the rules and features of computers, my drawing improved a lot. Soon I became one of the earliest artists in China using the computer to draw. During that time, when people talked about me, they always said, "Oh, the one who uses a computer…" Eventually I ended up publishing several books to teach people how to use the computer to draw.

Has Painter helped you to define your own style?

Before Painter, CG was considered a tool for commercial design—like architecture, technical drawing, textile design, and commercial illustration. I tried using several different drawing programs, but CG gave my work too much of a "computer feeling"—a feeling of coldness and redundant patterns.

Once I found out that Painter had good, traditional drawing-imitation possibilities, I began to use it. I still use Painter to imitate oil and watercolor painting styles for comic books. This kind of comic book creation allows me, as an artist, a greater intimacy with the tool.

Also, before I started using Painter, my drawings were in black and white. Using Painter has helped me become a colorful artist and illustrator, and I use it for my entire creative process.

What motivates you?

From the beginning, my talent and passion for painting pushed me to lay down everything I saw on paper. I was obsessed by the painting technique. But soon this desire was replaced by a passion for expressing what I think. After I graduated from school and had a social life, I was shocked by the craziness and absurdity of society. The thoughts of people are far more crazy and scary than the reality. I wish to express, through drawing, inner human struggles.

Which artists do you admire and why?

I admire Boucq, Bilal, Frezzato, and Guarnido. They are not just artists, but charming personalities. I think the greatest art in the world is the personality of the artist. An artist with a boring personality will have no chance to create great works. The great artists are always somehow great philosophers, too, so I like the special personality of these artists.

How has the Internet influenced your art-making process?

The Internet is important; 10 years ago, no magazine wanted to publish my work, let alone publish my books. So I just drew on the computer and uploaded my work to the Internet for free. It made quite a little sensation because, at that time, the Chinese weren't at all familiar with color comics and realistic digital drawings. People began to spread the word about my work. My debut with my audience was really on the Internet.

Is there anything else that you would like to share with us?

Artists always indulge in their own worlds; as a matter of fact, the nature of art is creating illusions. It is like smoking weed: people like to find the illusion they fancy to escape from reality. This is a great thing. Human beings as physically existing in the world are full of dissatisfactions. But their spirit can hang around in the art world. The feelings are very real sometimes; they can bring you joy, which makes you wonder about the meaning of the existence in the real world. Artists stand in the starting point of the desire and disappointment of human beings. They hold the key to solving pains. Sometimes artists exaggerate their own value, however, without the resonance of people, and as illusion makers, what would be the value of their creations? Art that fails to leave an impression on others— not reaching even one or two persons— is art without meaning.

Resources

On the DVD

- Art Gallery

Links

- http://blog.sina.com.cn/benjamin
- http://www.youtube.com
- http://www.youku.com

BENJAMIN

Education

Fashion Design degree

Client List

Xiao Pan Publishing House (France), Marvel Comics (USA), La Rinascente (Italy), Universal Music

Awards and Career Highlights

2000: First works published

2004: Golden Dragon Award (1st National Comic Award in China)

2008: The Best Comic Book of 2008 (France); solo exhibition in Arludik, Paris

Gallery

"Alien on Earth."

"Little Girl."

"Hatred (1)."

"Hatred (2)."

COMIC BOOK ILLUSTRATION

"Hatred (3)."

"Long Hu Men (Dragon and Tiger)."

"Jena Lee (1)."

"Jena Lee (2)."

"Catwoman."

"The Shining Leaving Away."

YOUCHAN

About the Artist

I was born in 1968 in Nishio City, Aichi Prefecture, Japan. After graduating from the Nagoya Sogo Design College, I began working at a design firm. Later I became a freelance illustrator, and in 2000 I established Toguru Company, Ltd. My artistic repertoire generally encompasses science fiction and fantasy illustrations, but past commissions have covered a variety of genres—including book covers, information pamphlets, and publications targeting families, Web sites, sales promotions, and corporate calendars. Since 2006, I have been exhibiting a series of personal works titled *Bungaku Sanbo.* The series features my illustrations of fantasy novels and science fiction works. I am a member of Illustrator E Space, the Society of Children's Book Writers & Illustrators, and the Japanese Science Fiction (SF) Writers Club. I currently live in Yokohama, Japan.

Artist's Statement

Where work is concerned, my priorities are to meet deadlines and to have a clear understanding of what the client wants from me. In terms of artistic expression, I try to create work that is atmospheric and full of nuances.

Influences

I frequently draw inspiration from music and books. My artistic drive goes up when I come across inspirational novels or music. Rather than illustrations or paintings, I find myself being touched by other medium of expression.

YOUCHAN

Studio

Software: Painter, Illustrator, Photoshop, Windows Vista

Hardware: Dell Studio 540, Wacom Intuos 4

Contact

Youchan ▪ Togoru Company, Ltd. ▪ Yokohama City, Japan
sales@togoru.net ▪ http://www.youchan.com

"Black Clock" Inspired by Steve Erickson's *Tours of the Black Clock.*

Techniques

Step-by-Step Tutorial: Masking

My inspiration for this piece is William Gibson's political thriller, *Spook Country*.

1. I begin in Illustrator by drawing my original image. I choose somber colors to reflect the darkly satirical feeling of Gibson's novel. See Figure 9.1. When I am satisfied with my image, I save the file in (Photoshop) PSD format and retain the original layers. I export the file into Painter.

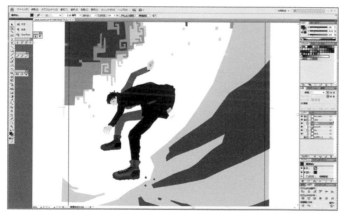

Figure 9.1   Create the initial drawing in Illustrator.

2. I open my PSD image file in Painter. I choose the Magic Wand tool and make sure Contiguous is checked. I use the Magic Wand to select the area I want to work in. See Figure 9.2.

Figure 9.2   Open in Painter and use the Magic Wand to select an area.

3. In Figure 9.3, I add color to create texture inside the selected area. I mainly use Acrylics, Dry Brush 30 for this step. I use the Color Wheel and follow my instincts when choosing colors.

Figure 9.3   Paint with Acrylics Dry Brush to create texture.

Figure 9.4   Select multiple areas to work in by using the Shift key.

4. To select multiple areas containing the same color at the same time, I use the Magic Wand and click on the color I want while pressing the Shift key. I also have the option to uncheck the Contiguous box, but if I do this, I might accidentally end up selecting areas outside my chosen color. See Figure 9.4.

5. In Figure 9.5 I add tonal gradations by painting directly over the surface with Acrylics Dry Brush 30. I use a color that has a middle value without selecting the relevant areas.

6. Once I am satisfied with my image, I save it in TIF format. Figure 9.6 shows the final image.

Figure 9.5   Add visual interest by blending over lines.

Figure 9.6 "Spook" final image.

Insights

The Creative Process

I begin my illustrations using Illustrator; I make a drawing that serves as the basis of my illustration, and I export it in PSD format. Next, using Painter, I add different textures and gradations to my drawing to further refine and polish the work. The finishing touches that I add in Painter are an important part of all my images.

Favorite Features

My favorite Painter tool, and the one I use the most, is the Acrylics Dry Brush. This brush reproduces the acrylic "touch" that I am familiar with from my days of working with traditional acrylic paints.

Timesaving Tips

I learn about the tools in Painter by using them regularly. This way I don't lose a lot of time while working by being unsure about what tools to utilize.

Finished Work

For private or group exhibitions, I print out my work and frame it for display. I print my illustrations on an ink-jet printer at home for any work up to a SuperA3 size. I also upload images onto my Web site for online exhibition. When finishing an image, I am aware of the discrepancy between what the public wants to see and what I want to express. Like steering a gigantic ship, I try to gradually swing the public around to the way I want to express myself.

Q&A

When did you start using Painter?

I first remember trying out Painter when it was in version 4, and then I purchased version 5.

What do you wish someone had told you when you started?

In the beginning, I wish someone had told me about color matching, resolution, and file formats. (For example, the RIF format is not commonly used.)

Did you have previous experience in traditional media?

Yes, I have worked with acrylic gesso on watercolor paper.

Has Painter helped you define your own style?

Painter's range of expressions really comes into its own when adding depth or nuance to a drawing.

Which artists do you admire?

I admire the writer Kurt Vonnegut. When life becomes unbearably difficult or sad, his carefully woven words and thoughts provide the perfect antidote for my feelings—like puzzle pieces that fit together.

How has the Internet influenced your art-making process?

I use the Internet as a public relations platform—it is an effective method of communication for advertising my work. The Internet is also useful for collecting reference materials. Of course, not everything I come across is genuine, so I don't jump to conclusions, and I try to collect as much information as I can.

What advice do you have for artists working with Painter?

Painter comes with a huge range of tools; find one or two that work for you. Painter is like an art shop; you don't need to familiarize yourself with everything.

Resources

On the DVD

- Artist Gallery

Links

- http://togoru.net
- http://www.youchan.com
- http://www.youchan.com/e-space/youchan_e.html
- http://www.scbwi.org/

YOUCHAN

Education

Nagoya Sogo Design College

Client List

Rironsha; Japan Broadcast Publishing Co., Ltd.; Kaisei Publishing; Kenkyusha Co., Ltd.; Hayakawa Shobo; SOFTBANK Creative Corp.; Hon no Zasshi sha; Gijutsu-Hyohron Co., Ltd.; Sekai Bunka Publishing Inc.; Kumon Publishing Co. Ltd.; Nagaokashoten Ltd.

Awards and Career Highlights

2006: Ballistic Publishing's Painter—The World's Finest Painter Art award

2009: Winner of 20th Reader's award, Illustrator Division of *SF Magazine* published by Hayakawa Shobo

Gallery

"Jajauma." Inspired by Mio Fou's *Jajauma*.

"Emerger." Inspired by Yukihiro Takahashi's *Emerger*.

ILLUSTRATION

"Quid." Inspired by Ray Bradbury's *Quid Pro Quo.*

"Snowman." Inspired by Norman Lock's *Land of the Snow Men.*

PETE REVONKORPI

About the Artist

I have been drawing my whole life but, professionally, I started to paint quite late—at around the age of 22.

I have always wanted to be a writer and tell stories. When I realized that the kinds of stories I wanted to tell were what people call "children's stories," I also realized that I would need illustrations. So I decided to learn how to illustrate—to learn how to tell stories through pictures. Since then, my works have been published in numerous Finnish newspapers and magazines. I have also created other illustrated works, such as CD cover art.

In 2009, I started working with a musician to produce what we call "living and singing paintings." They combine live digital painting with live music to tell a story without words. At this point, we have only performed here in Finland, but we hope to take our performances abroad in the future.

Artist's Statement

I adore simplicity, and I try not to put anything extra in my paintings—only what is absolutely necessary. I try to strip my thoughts and emotions completely naked. Although I often use clever concepts in my paintings, they are not really what the painting is all about. It is all about the emotion the painting evokes—or doesn't evoke. For example, I can use the color blue to create a sad feeling in the painting, but I can also use a sad concept to do that. The concept of a painting is really just another one of its colors.

Influences

Anything can be inspirational. As long as you can see the invisible side of things, there is magic everywhere.

PETE REVONKORPI

Studio

    Software: Painter

    Hardware: Wacom Intuos 4

Contact

    Pete Revonkorpi ▪ Jyväskylä, Finland ▪ peterevonkorpi@hotmail.com ▪ http://peterevonkorpi.daportfolio.com

"On the Pier."

Techniques

Step-by-Step Tutorial: Smoothing

I don't do a lot of tricks with Painter—I just paint. One thing that I do often is what I call *smoothing*. After I have painted something, I take the Thick Wet Oils 30 Brush and reduce its opacity to almost 0 (usually 4–6). I then pick a color that I have used a lot in the painting and just paint all over it. This smoothes the image and gives it a soft and painted look that I like a lot. I usually do this separately to different sections and objects in the painting while I work.

1. In Figure 10.1, the edges of the woman's hair and her dress are clear to see. I use the Oils, Thick Wet Oils 30 Brush and reduce its opacity to 6. I choose a color that I have already used to paint with in the section that I want to smooth (in this case, green for the hair and orange for the dress) and paint carelessly all over it.

2. The result is a much softer image, with a much more painterly look. I use this smoothing technique in practically every one of my paintings to give them a soft and dreamlike quality.

TIP

I use Painter pretty much the same way I would paint in real life: I just pick up a brush and start painting. This is exactly why I like Painter so much—it allows my personal style to come through naturally.

Figure 10.1 Smoothing over the hair and dress.

Figure 10.2 "The Gardener" final image.

Insights

The Creative Process

I often start with little idea of what I am going to do. I might have a certain shade of color that I want to use—but anything beyond that is a mystery to me. I usually just start to slam colors and shapes together without care, and pretty soon some blob of color starts looking like something—maybe a boat. Next, I ask myself questions about the boat. Is the boat sinking? Is it just drifting, or is it going somewhere? Who are the passengers? And so on. So, actually, I don't really *paint* a painting; I just try to *find* it under all that white.

> **TIP**
>
> As an illustrator, the most important thing to me is that the image gives new life to the text it illustrates—that it gives a new and clear angle to the subject matter and evokes emotion or thought.

Favorite Features

In Painter, I use mostly the oil and acrylic brushes—especially the Thick Wet Oil and Wet Acrylic Brushes. I like the textures I get and the way colors blend with the oil brushes.

Timesaving Tips

Two of my biggest and simplest timesavers have been to learn the shortcut keys for the actions I use the most and to use as many layers as possible when I paint.

These may seem like obvious things to do, but for someone like me, who usually starts painting without advance thought, they are things I have to constantly try to remember—especially when I am working on an illustration for a client. For instance, if a client wants an object to be on the right side of the image rather than on the left side, by using layers and shortcut keys, I can simply move the object to the right and show my client what it will look like. Having everything painted in different layers helps me a lot when adjusting the image later on—this way I don't have to repaint the entire image.

Finished Work

My finished work is usually displayed either printed on paper or as an image on the Internet.

Q&A

When did you start using Painter?

I started using Painter about six years ago.

Do you integrate your work in Painter with traditional artists' materials?

No, I do all my work in Painter—from start to finish.

How has it been for you to learn about using art tools in a digital setting?

Learning is easy in a digital environment because it is so flexible. I find it is much easier to experiment digitally than using traditional art materials.

Has Painter helped you define your own style?

Like I said, Painter has helped me experiment. The painting process is so fast and flexible, compared to traditional media, that it is much easier to try different things. Also, using Painter is much cheaper because you don't have to buy new canvases, brushes, and paints after you have wasted them on failed experiments. With Painter, you can afford to fail as many times as you want.

What motivates you?

I am motivated by the need to understand and explain. My works, or at least my personal works, are very personal. But I try to turn the personal into universal. And I am interested in the invisible side of life: things that are lost, and things that are not yet found. For example, a chair, no matter how beautifully crafted it may be, is not that interesting. But an empty chair—the fact that there is nobody sitting there—now that is interesting and inspiring! Why is it empty? Has somebody just left, or was there someone who never arrived? I don't think I could ever paint a still life of fruits in a bowl, but I would probably be ecstatic to paint just the bowl. So I guess you could say that I try to visualize the invisible.

Which artists do you admire?

My single biggest influence has been Astrid Lindgren, although she was not an illustrator, but an author. Her book *Ronia the Robber's Daughter* was the first book that I remember reading as a child and the first children's book I reread as an adult. When I reread it some years ago, I literally cried through all the pages—it was that powerful. I knew then that telling "children's stories" through pictures was what I wanted to do—that illustration had to be the most powerful form, or style, of art there was.

And it wasn't just because of the nostalgia, but because the simplicity and naivety help people to let their guard down. Most people don't expect anything other than pretty colors and whimsy from a children's book. As a result, deep and complex emotions come as a complete surprise and are therefore more powerful.

Illustrators who I admire a lot are Tove Jansson, creator of *The Moomins*, and Maurice Sendak, who is, perhaps, the greatest living illustrator. I also adore the work of artists Marc Chagall and Frida Kahlo. These kinds of artists have helped me understand how much you can say with very little.

How has the Internet influenced your art-making process?
The Internet has influenced me quite a lot. Without the Internet, I would have to travel across the world to see what other people are doing, but now I can do it from my home with just a mouse click. The Internet is an endless source of inspiration.

What advice do you have for artists working with Painter?
Experiment. Take time to fiddle around with different settings. This way you will eventually find your own unique way of doing things, and your images will have your own unique look. This is what is so great about Painter—it allows your personal style to really come through. There is already enough clean generic digital art out there!

Resources

On the DVD
- Artist Gallery

Links
- http://peterevonkorpi.daportfolio.com
- http://www.youtube/user/PeteRevonkorpi

Gallery

"Dreams of Flying."

"Starfisher."

ILLUSTRATION

"Going to Sleep."

"Together."

"The Boy with Bees in His Hair."

PETE REVONKORPI

"Her Majesty."

ILLUSTRATION

"Stairs."

"A Sea for the Ones Who Can't Swim."

TORSTEN WOLBER

About the Artist

I studied at the Cologne International School of Design with a focus on illustration. Over the past 12 years, I have worked as an illustrator, and I switched to digital painting in 2004. Since then I have won several prizes for my digital artwork, including the Painter Master award from Ballistic, first and third place prizes in the CG Challenge, the German International Docma award, and the Corel Painter award. Most of my work reflects daily commissions for advertising, magazines, TV, and games. These include *stern*, *FOCUS*, *WirtschaftsWoche*, *Playboy*, Jung von Matt, WDR, Blue Byte, and KARAKTER Concepts.

Artist's Statement

Frankly, I've never completely understood the mystery that people make about being an artist. I think that if you have a vision and the strong urge to share it, it's merely a matter of time and hard work to find a unique way to express yourself. Tools like Painter make it easy for me to transform my painting experience into the digital world, which leads me to new inspirations by other artists, a still joyful game in which it is fun to learn from each other. I'm grateful every day to have this wonderful profession.

Influences

It's hard to say what my direct influences are, because I always try to keep an open mind to all different influences in art. I have never developed a truly unique illustrative style, so there are a still a lot of artists from different corners of the world who influence me, and I enjoy this freedom. Because of this, my range of illustrative styles is probably a little broader than that of most other artists.

TORSTEN WOLBER

Studio

Software: Painter, Photoshop, and sometimes SketchUp for perspective

Hardware: MacPro, Quato Intelli Proof monitor, Wacom Intuos 4 A4

Contact

Torsten Wolber ▪ Cologne, Germany ▪ online@torstenwolber.de ▪ http://www.torstenwolber.de

"Exodus of the Tree Elves."

Techniques

Step-by-Step Tutorial: "Trophies"

1. I begin by drawing a small sketch of my idea. By small, I mean that my doodle is not more than 5 inches in height on my screen. I use the regular Acrylics, Opaque Detail Brush 3, and every now and then, I alter it to an ellipsoid shape by changing the angle and form. To prevent losing my vision of the drawing, I work as fast as I can at this stage. It shouldn't take more than an hour and a half to complete this first step. I don't limit myself by focusing on details right now. It's the big picture I'm looking for. See Figure 11.1.

2. After I decide that I like the colors, I check on the overall composition using the Divine Proportions tool and the Layout Grid. See Figures 11.2 and 11.3. I often do this right after blocking things out so I get a better idea of balancing out all the elements in my image. I start pushing things around using the Lasso tool and do some "paint-overs." Every piece of artwork results from decisions to be made, and grids and proportions help me to easily get on track. However, I take them as loose guidelines rather than relying on them too heavily.

3. In Figure 11.4, I enlarge my initial sketch. Using the Sargent Brush tool with default settings, I do a paint-over, as seen in Figure 11.5. Using this technique is the easiest way to define wrinkles.

Figure 11.1   Initial sketch.

> ## NOTE
>
> **Even during the earliest stages of designing your image, you can get helpful hints from Painter by using the Divine Proportions tool or the Layout Grid to check your composition.**

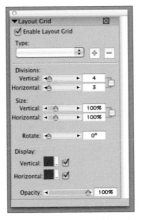

Figure 11.3 Layout Grid settings.

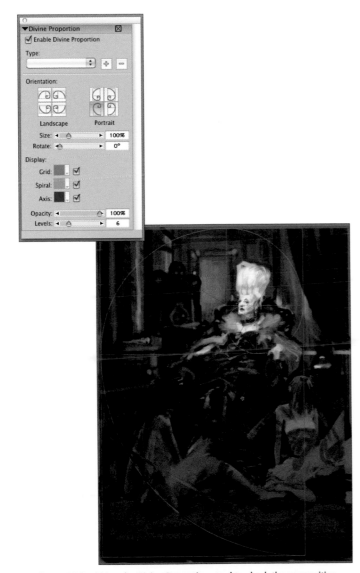

Figure 11.2 Using the Divine Proportions tool to check the composition.

Figure 11.4 Initial sketch.

ILLUSTRATION

Figure 11.5   Paint-over with Sargent Brush.

4. After Dodging, I work on the details with a Fine Oil Brush. See Figure 11.6.

Figure 11.6   Dodging and detailing.

5. After detailing each element of my picture individually (see Figure 11.7), I combine all the parts again onto a new canvas, adjust some of the colors and positions, and then Drop All into one background. See Figure 11.8. In Figure 11.9, I have combined all the different parts of my image into one layer and over-painted them using the Sargent Brush.

NOTE

I know that combining all parts of my image into a single layer isn't a common way to work, but because I am used to working on one canvas only, this has certain benefits. For example, I can concentrate on my work without bothering to check whether I'm working in the right layer. Even more important is the fact that the formerly separated objects begin to interact with each other once again— this includes the fuzzy edges and all. Maybe it's just my "analog habit," but I definitely encourage you to try to get out of "safety mode" by trying this.

Figure 11.7 Elements separated and rendered.

ILLUSTRATION

Figure 11.8 Drop All into a new single layer.

6. At this point I decide to add a textured layer to my image.
I add a brushed texture but erase it in certain areas where
it appears to be too dominant; it's easy to overdo this.
See Figure 11.10. I add the texture in a separate layer with
Brushwork On in Overlay mode and adjust the Layer
Opacity to approximately 20 percent. See Figure 11.11.

TIP

I often add a textured layer in the final stages of my work
because it helps me avoid a digital look that, especially
when printed, appears to be a tad too clean and smooth.

Figure 11.9 Elements recombined onto one canvas.

Figure 11.10   Partially erased brush texture.

Figure 11.11   Overlay in 100 percent.

7. I finalize the picture with another Overlay layer, where I add some highlights and shadows. See Figure 11.12. While in Overlay mode, I also alter the colors where needed. I Drop All Layers again and sharpen the final image just a little bit. Now I'm done.

Figure 11.12 Texture and additional overlay.

Figure 11.13 "Trophies" final image.

Insights

The Creative Process

To begin, I need something to start working with, so I start sketching right away. My first sketches are almost always bad. (Really, I mean it!) Once I have my idea sketched out in Painter, I check my composition using the Divine Proportion tool and the Layout Grid. After that, I start painting over the top of my sketch.

Favorite Features

If there was one tool I would really miss in a world without Painter, it would be the Sargent Brush. You can see the difference in brushstrokes by comparing Figure 11.14 to Figure 11.15. Most people rarely use the Sargent Brush because it feels like playing the piano with a pair of boxing gloves on. Yet this is exactly the randomness I look for; it helps trigger my imagination. Even when using traditional analog techniques, I often needed this type of unpredictable factor that would lead to "happy accidents." For example, I often started painting with a broad clumsy brush or worked left-handed.

Figure 11.14
Painted with regular Oil Brush.

Figure 11.15
Painted with the Sargent Brush.

Timesaving Tips

Use fewer brushes! Keep your brushes organized and few, and use Arrange Palettes to save your sets. See Figure 11.16. Beginners are often inclined to work with way too many brushes and sometimes find themselves getting lost in all the possibilities. I have 3 different brush sets for different techniques; each of them contains not more than 12 brushes. See Figure 11.17. This way it's easy for me to locate everything quickly and easily without getting distracted.

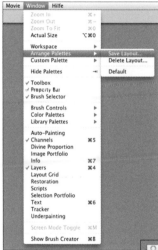

Figure 11.16
Organize brush sets in Arrange Palettes.

Figure 11.17   Use fewer brushes.

Finished Work

My finished work is usually printed in magazines or advertisements. My biggest concern with my finished work is, "Hmm...when will I be paid?"

Q&A

When did you start using Painter?

I started using Painter, along with Photoshop, in 2003.

What do you wish someone had told you when you started?

I wish someone had told me that Painter has some issues with color management. Tip: stick with Adobe RGB and PSD files in both Painter and Photoshop.

Did you have previous experience in traditional media?

I have had lots of experience with traditional media. Soon after graduating, I began working as an illustrator using traditional tools. I worked this way for 13 years. Sometimes I integrate my work in Painter with traditional artists' materials by adding some traditionally made structures.

How has it been for you to learn about using art tools in a digital setting?

It's been surprisingly easy!

Has Painter helped you define your own style?

In a way, yes, Painter has helped with this. Although I never really worked to develop my own style, Painter has helped me stick with my own traditional painting style. I love to work painterly and loose, although I have to admit that's not always what the client wants.

What motivates you?

I am always motivated and inspired after I share my vision with others. Feedback from my peers is still providing me with, by far, the strongest motivation I have for my work.

How has the Internet influenced your art-making process?

The Internet is a great way to get useful references and find inspiration, but discussing your work with other experienced digital artists is invaluable. I definitely recommend finding a community of peers to share thoughts and questions with. Two of my favorite sites are the German Illustrators Organization Web site and the German DigitalArtForum (led by the very professional Daniel Lieske, who gives away all his knowledge for free).

What advice do you have for artists working with Painter?

Don't get lost in the possibilities. Put on your blinders, and concentrate on just one problem at a time.

Resources

On the DVD

- Artist Gallery

Links

- http://www.io-home.org
- http://www.torstenwolber.de
- http://www.digitalartforum.de

TORSTEN WOLBER

Education

Illustration degree

Client List

stern; FOCUS; WirtschaftsWoche; Playboy; Jung von Matt; WDR; Blue Byte; KARAKTER Concepts

Awards and Career Highlights

Ballistic: Painter Master award; 2006 and 2007 CG award; Docma award; Corel Painter award; Arno award

TORSTEN WOLBER

ILLUSTRATION

Gallery

"Anno 1404—Harbour."

"Anno 1404—Sultan's Palace."

TORSTEN WOLBER

"Window."

"War of the Worlds."

"EON—Book Cover."

"Pin-Up."

"Campaign—Bosch Kitchen."

ILLUSTRATION

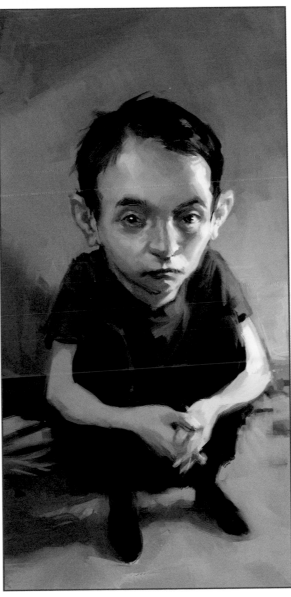

"Speedpaint."

JEAN-LUC TOUILLON

About the Artist

I was born on October 19, 1949, in Paris, France. Ever since I was 5 years old, I wanted to be an artist. When I was a teen, I would rather have been given an art book on Delacroix than a new suit (when my mother gave me the choice). By my teens, I was already considered to be a creative person at all the schools that I attended. In 1968, I entered the National School of Decorative Arts in Paris (ENSAD-Paris), but only after succeeding in passing the competitive exam. Of the 1,500 candidates taking the exam, I was among the 30 successful students.

Sensing the development of the computer for use in the field of visual arts, I joined the Apple France Graphic Studio in 1986. In 1988 I, along with my long-time friend Gilles Audoux, organized a live drawing performance in the Visconti Gallery in Paris. All of the Paris art press and media agents were there to see me draw a live portrait using a computer mouse. Since then, I have participated in many Digital Creator's Nights worldwide. I still perform live drawing shows with my Wacom tablet at various events and fairs. In January 2010, I performed at the Angoulême International Comics Festival. As an art teacher I have, most notably, taught at the School of Visual Communication in the Rue de Sèvres (ECV-Paris) and at the National School of Fine Arts in Paris (ENSBA-Paris). I am the founding member of three companies: Digital Patchwork in 1995; la F@ktory in 1996; and Art-canes in 2005—where I am still the creative director today.

Artist's Statement

I try to capture realities and integrate them into my dreamlike worlds, creating encounters between fantasy, the virtual world, and the real world.

Influences

The things that influence me are my background, my memories, my dreams, and the computer world. I also feel the influence of the great masters of art and their techniques.

Photo : D.Gadoin

JEAN-LUC TOUILLON

Studio

Software: Painter, Live Picture, Photoshop, Illustrator, Motion, After Effects

Hardware: MacPro, MacBook Pro, Wacom Intuos 4, and Cintiq 21UX

Contact

Jean-Luc Touillon ■ ART-canes ■ Issy-les-Moulineaux, France
jeanluctouillon@me.com ■ http://www.touillon.com

"Encre Rouge"

Techniques

Step-by-Step Tutorial: Aquatint-Style Portrait

This is a drawing that I created using multiple Liquid Ink and Watercolor layers. My goal in creating this portrait is to obtain the same effect as that of an aquatint.

> **NOTE**
>
> In a traditional engraving process, the *burr side* is the incised side of a copper plate. The copper shavings, known as the burr, are then cleaned from the plate before it is inked.

> **NOTE**
>
> *Aquatint* is an intaglio printmaking technique in which acid "bites" into a metal plate, usually copper or zinc. This etching process produces a design that consists of tonal areas rather than lines.

1. In Painter, I select New Liquid Ink Layer and, using my Wacom tablet, I draw the portrait of a woman. Next, I duplicate my drawing in a new layer. I then select New Watercolor Layer in the Menu palette to provide the anchor for the burr side, as in an engraving. See Figure 12.1.

Figure 12.1　Use Liquid Inks to draw the portrait.

2. As I paint, I continue to use the same technique and move the work area to duplicate watercolor layers. I create painted textures using the Watercolor, Runny Airbrush. I make variations of the different layers, always changing the opacity and blending modes. See Figure 12.2.

Figure 12.3   Fill some areas with Liquid Watercolors.

Figure 12.2   Create textured layers with the Airbrush tool.

3. In Figure 12.3, I use a custom Watercolors Brush to add large transparent spots of red to stain the surface of the image.

4. I finish it by adding black watercolor for contrast. My goal in this image is to create the effect of an aquatint. See Figure 12.4.

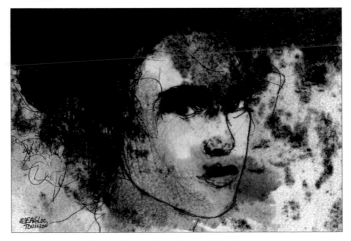

Figure 12.4   "Portrait Grave" final image.

ILLUSTRATION

Insights

The Creative Process

My creative process includes many sketches and drawings from life that are then enriched by interpretation steps and integration with a pattern or a texture—depending on the story I want to tell.

Favorite Features

My favorite Painter features are the sketching tools—pencils, inks, paints, and watercolor. I can create the paper textures myself.

Customizable Tools

I create many custom tools for myself in Painter based on textures that I scan, after I've invented them using traditional art materials. I also design custom paper textures to control the Texture Brushes on my canvas. In addition, I make custom stain marks. For example, using my own tools, I paint stains, such as in Figure 12.5, that then serve as the basis for building my custom tools.

Figure 12.5   A custom stain mark
created using Oils.

Timesaving Tips

A big timesaver is the configuration of my Wacom tablet keyboard, which I adapt to the work I am doing. Another timesaver is the integration of new and custom keyboard shortcuts in the Preferences menu. I configure only one key on my tablet with three shortcuts: New File, Full Screen, and Start Script. I create these shortcuts in the Painter Preferences menu, and then I add the shortcuts to the tablet. I also use several tablet pens to save time because Painter links one tool to one pen. (I put colored signs on my pens so I can distinguish each of them.) Thus, I have a pencil pen, a quill pen, and a watercolor pen. Working this way also allows me to have different pressure settings, depending on each tool. I configure the top button on the pen with All Tool Windows and the bottom button with Space Bar (to get the Grabber tool).

Finished Work

My finished work is usually printed, displayed in galleries or on CD/DVD, or projected as motion graphics onto a screen for creating a live show performance. The rendering of colors and the display are what I consider to be most important when publishing my finished work.

Q&A

When did you start using Painter?

I started using Painter in 1991. At that time I was already a user of both ImageStudio and ColorStudio.

What do you wish someone had told you when you started?

I started in with the first version of Painter—and because I was already a user of ColorStudio, the transition came gently. At that time, I used to meet often with Mark Zimmer, one of the founders of Painter.

Did you have previous experience in traditional media?

I have had an academic background, and I practice both traditional and digital art—the one enriching the other. Traditional art materials that I have worked with include charcoal pencil, graphite pencil, ink drawing, watercolor, oil painting, gouache painting, acrylic painting, engraving, and pastel drawing.

Do you integrate your work in Painter with traditional artists' materials? How?

I sometimes integrate my work with the custom textures I have scanned. These textures are details of my traditionally created artworks.

Has Painter helped you define your own style?

I already had my graphic style before working on a computer, so I naturally transposed my own style using a digital media.

What motivates you?

Creation, imagination, experiments, and curiosity all motivate me.

Which artists do you admire?

I admire Michelangelo, Rembrandt, Goya, Giandomenico Tiepolo, Auguste Rodin, Egon Schiele, and Francis Bacon for their discourses and for the way they mastered their art.

How has the Internet influenced your art-making process?

The Internet gives me a way to transmit my artwork worldwide and allows me to inform myself.

What advice do you have for artists working with Painter?

Draw, and keep drawing continuously.

ILLUSTRATION

Resources

On the DVD

- Artist Gallery
- Illustrated Animations

Links

- http://www.touillon.com
- http://www.gadoin.com
- http://www.gillesaudoux.com
- http://www.awn.com/toccafondo
- http://www.michaelhussar.biz/pages/main_menu_pg.html
- http://www.ballisticpublishing.com
- http://beinart.org/viewtopic.php?t=1317
- http://www.rickberrystudio.com
- http://www.beksinski.pl
- http://www.pignon-ernest.com

JEAN-LUC TOUILLON

Education

1972 École Nationale Supérieure des Arts Décoratifs, Paris France—graphic arts, engraving, fresco, and mosaic

Client List

Ungaro; Chanel; Hermès; Opéra de Paris; Suma; Banque Populaire; EDF-GDF; Auchan; Alfa-Laval; Davigel; ICI; Nasa; CEE; Regain; Moët & Chandon; Vinchon Jeanette; Connexion; Sopra; Solo Moteurs; Région Emilia-Romagna; BDDP; Bouygues Télécom; Denis & Co; Forum Européen pour la Sécurité Urbaine; Laval-Virtual; INRA; Parfum d'image; Wanadoo; Mister Co.

Awards and Career Highlights

1986–1996: Apple France Graphic Studio

Instructor at the National School of Fine Arts (ENSBA) in Paris

Gold Medal—Sculpture, Saint-Rémy-les-Chevreuses

Wacom expert/consultant; Corel Painter Master

Selected Shows

Salon des Illustrateurs (Paris); 89 Artistes Prennent la Bastille (Paris);

Exhibitions at: Artom (Clermont-Ferrand); Le Verre à Pied (Paris); Profils (Collioure); Micro-Buss (Clermont-Ferrand); VidéoFormes (Clermont-Ferrand); National School of Fine Arts (Saint-Etienne); National School of Fine Arts (Toulon); Fort-de-France Festival (Martinique); Museum of Dignes-les-Bains; 55 Mercer Gallery (New York)

International 3D fair "Imagina" (Monaco); Latino American Congress, Quito (Ecuador); International 3D fair, Malmö (Sweden); Digital Creators' Nights: Paris, Milan, Barcelona, London, Stockholm, San Francisco

Three dedicated programs are on French television channels.

Gallery

"Bleu Serenissime."

"Femme Chalk."

"Aqua Elle."

"Bateau Trois Femmes."

"Blanche."

"Monsieur Clown."

"Soir Serenissime."

"Mouche."

CHET PHILLIPS

About the Artist

I present my slightly off-center view of the world through my digital illustrations. I received a BFA in painting and drawing (with a heavy influence from the printmaking department) in 1979 and then ventured into the world of commercial illustration. In 1992, my traditional illustration tools were replaced by a computer and Painter version 1. Painter has now become my primary tool for creating digital woodcuts and scratchboard-style images. I create illustrations for advertising, design, publishing, editorial, and corporate clients—and as usual, no electrons are harmed in the process.

Artist's Statement

As an illustrator, my focus of creation is the interpretation of ideas, thoughts, and stories. I've pursued this way of working for years as an interpreter of other people's words and have recently begun the practice of creating worlds of characters and visual stories from my own ideas as self-published projects.

Influences

My artwork is influenced by popular culture and surrealism with a large dose of humor thrown in. Incongruities in life and stories that may have many meanings also intrigue me. Exploring these areas with my artwork is a constant source of inspiration.

Artists that I admire include Rockwell Kent, Edgar Degas, Henri de Toulouse-Lautrec, René Magritte, Charles Addams, Steve Ditko, and Jack Kirby—they all find a truly unique voice in their creations that I naturally resonate with.

CHET PHILLIPS

Studio

Software: Painter, Photoshop, Illustrator, InDesign

Hardware: 27-inch iMac Core i5

Contact

Chet Phillips ■ Chet Phillips Illustration ■ Texas, USA ■ chet@chetart.com ■ http://www.chetart.etsy.com ■ http://www.chetart.com

"Billy Goats Gruff."

Techniques

Step-by-Step Tutorial: Creating a Steampunk Monkey Trading Card

Inspired by turn-of-the-century cigarette cards, the predecessor to modern-day sports and entertainment trading cards, I've recently been exploring a world of monkey-related themes. First came the "World War Monkey" series, which is a blend of military general portraits from the Victorian era matched with simian characteristics. I've just released a series on monkeys and apes that form a world of a secret cabal of evil, known as the "Society of Sinister Simians." Sandwiched between the two sets is a collection of Steampunk-inspired characters—one of which is highlighted in this technique. Steampunk is a subgenre of speculative fiction and fantasy that became well known during the 1980s and early 1990s. The term specifically refers to works set in a time or place where steam power is still widely used—for example, the 19th century or Victorian-era England—and includes science fiction, or fantasy elements, such as fictional technological inventions much like the ones found in the works of Jules Verne and H. G. Wells.

The character Ezekiel M. Nightshade is a portrait of a baboon demonstrating the characteristics of the above-described Steampunk culture. In a top hat, with Victorian-styled garb, he is outfitted with industrial-age items that are slightly skewed toward a futuristic alternative universe. His brief biography reads:

Psychic Detective

Famed for communicating with the dead and solving cases of misplaced and troubled souls. His invention, the Ecto-Plasmoid Specter-Mometer Tell-All Scope, *was a key tool in enhancing his natural-born abilities. Shortly after solving his 1000th case, he walked into the Whispering Waterfall and was never seen again.*

Here is the creation of Ezekiel M. Nightshade in the style of scratchboard:

1. After some preliminary thumbnails and research for the type of monkey to use, I create a somewhat detailed sketch, using the parameters of my trading card size and shape. The only noncomputer component that has remained in my work is the sketching stage. I still enjoy the feel of pencil on paper when I'm working out the details of a piece. See Figure 13.1.

Figure 13.1   Create a detailed sketch.

Figure 13.2   Clone in Painter, and use transparency as a guide.

2. In Figure 13.2, I've scanned the sketch and opened it in Painter. I create a clone so that I can refer to my sketch with the transparency feature to use as a guide. I turn this feature on and off throughout the black-and-white line art stage as needed.

3. In Figure 13.3, I use the Scratchboard tool to create a black-and-white image from my sketch.

ILLUSTRATION

Figure 13.3 Line art is created in black and white.

Figure 13.4 Keep the line drawing as a separate layer.

4. Once I finish my line art, I click on the image with the Layer Adjuster tool and click Select All. This action creates a duplicate layer that shows only my line work with a blank, white layer underneath as my base. Next, I select my line art layer and change its Layer Composite Method in the Layers palette to Gel. Now all the white areas of my artwork are clear—as if the line work had been printed on a clear gel sheet. I lock the Gel layer to avoid accidentally adding color to it and select my background layer for coloring. I finish the area using the Paper Texture, Micron Grain, with Random Brush Stroke Grain turned off. I apply this hard-edged texture to give it a bit of a lithograph-printed feel, much like some old cigarette cards have. See Figure 13.4.

5. The first stage of coloring for this piece starts with a full Paint Bucket fill of the area with a cream color to knock down the bright white background. Next, I use the Pastels, Artist Pastel Chalk Brush, as seen in Figure 13.5. In the General palette, I select the Method: Cover, and Subcategory: Grainy Hard Cover and use a variety of paper textures, including Rock and Acid Etch. See Figure 13.6. Using this setup of Pastels Brush and settings, I work areas of the background to give it an aged, weathered look with grays, variations of brown, and blue versions of gray.

Figure 13.5   Create an aged effect in the background.

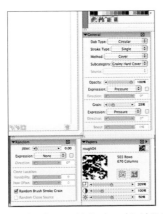

Figure 13.6   Use Grainy Cover with Rock and Acid Etch paper textures.

6. In Figure 13.7, I use the Lasso tool to create boundaries within the figure to apply color, protecting the background area.

NOTE

Using the Lasso tool in this manner is similar to the way I once used Frisket Paper, a thin adhesive-coated film (much like a giant sheet of Scotch tape), to mask off areas while using a traditional airbrush to paint.

The application of color is toggled between Random/On and Off in the Random palette radio button. With Random On, the texture fills in evenly and quickly. With Random Off, the texture is more defined and harder edged.

Figure 13.7   Use the Lasso tool to mask areas when adding color.

7. Next I will be adding some texture to the vest:

After researching some patterns that are appropriate for the Victorian period, I choose one to scan and utilize for the vest. In Figure 13.8, I save the pattern as a black-and-white file and then paste it into the image as a layer. In Figure 13.9, I use the Magic Wand (Tolerence-0 Continuous unchecked) to select all the black areas in the pattern. Once the selection is live, I eliminate the Pattern layer and choose the base layer. Using the Lasso tool, I hold the Option key down to remove areas of the selection that are not in the vest area. In Figure 13.10, the selection is feathered, and I apply color within it to define the pattern with darks and lights for highlights. See Figure 13.11.

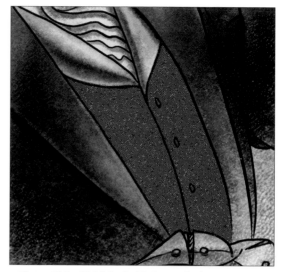

Figure 13.9　Highlight the black areas in the vest pattern.

Figure 13.8　Import texture for the vest.

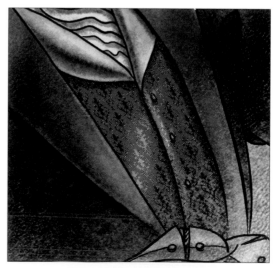

Figure 13.10　Feather the colors.

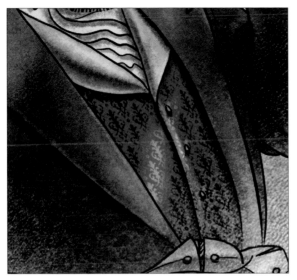

Figure 13.11 Create highlights in the fabric.

8. To give the image more of an aged look and feel, I work the bottom area with some textured light colors to fade it out. I do this with light colors on the base layers and white on the Line layer. See Figure 13.12.

9. I add text and a border to complete the image as a cigarette card. See Figure 13.13. Collect them all!

Figure 13.12 Use a lighter color at the bottom to age the image.

Figure 13.13   "Ezekiel M. Nightshade" final images.

Insights

The Creative Process

Once an idea sticks in my brain, I work up a series of small thumbnail sketches for compositional purposes. From there, I create one to three detailed sketches. Then I scan the final version to use as a tracing paper feature, which I go on to finish.

Favorite Features

The Scratchboard and Pastel Brushes, in conjunction with the tracing paper feature, are ones I use constantly. Working from a detailed sketch, I create a scratchboard feel to my art. Changing my black-and-white line art layer to Gel Composite in the Layers palette allows me to apply color on a lower level that shows through the "white" areas.

Customizable Tools

I use customizable tools in Painter mainly with hard grain and random paper textures when I add color to an image. I use the Artist Pastel Chalk Brush to apply color. Within the General palette area, the method I choose is Cover with Subcategory Grainy Hard Cover. In the Random palette, I alternate between the Random Brush Stroke Grain radio button turned off and on. This changes the character of texture applied from filling in with repeated strokes versus maintaining the same texture application in the same areas.

Finished Work

My finished work is usually displayed in printed material— magazines, books, trading cards, and framed prints. I consider color management to be the most important thing to consider when publishing my finished work.

Q&A

When did you start using Painter?

I started using Painter with version 1 in 1992.

What do you wish someone had told you when you started?

Go ahead and sell all your paints—you won't be using them again!

Did you have previous experience in traditional media?

I have worked with oil paints, gouache, color pencils, pen and ink, and traditional scratchboard. I have experience with the airbrush, besides lithography, etching, and woodcuts.

Has Painter helped you to define your own style?

Painter is an essential part of my creative process. Having worked with traditional tools beforehand, I find a wealth of extra time and flexibility to be inherent when using digital media. Painter has opened a level of experimentation, and trial and error, that was much slower in my previous traditional world of creation.

How has the Internet influenced your art-making process?

The Internet allows for a speedier process of sketch approval and art delivery.

What advice do you have for artists working with Painter?

If you are learning your art processes for the first time on a computer, you should take some time to explore traditional art tools as well.

Resources

On the DVD

- Artist Gallery

Links

- http://www.chetart.com
- http://drawn.ca
- http://www.etsy.com
- http://thelittlechimpsociety.com
- http://boingboing.net
- http://www.notcot.org

CHET PHILLIPS

Education

BFA painting and drawing; 30 years as a freelance commercial illustrator

Client List

American Airlines, ASPCA, Blue Cross Blue Shield, Bloomberg, Borders Books & Music, *Cricket Magazine*, The Dallas Morning News, Harcourt Brace, Hilton, Honda, Klutz Press, PepsiCo, *New York Times*, Prentice Hall, Warner Brothers, Workman Publishing

Awards and Career Highlights

1986–2000: Best of Show, Gold and Silver awards—Dallas Society of Illustrators

1993–2009: Macworld Art Expos

Showcased in a variety of digital art and illustration publications including *Painter Wow!*, *Spectrum*, *Expose*, *Print Magazine*, *Step Inside Design*, *Corel's Official Painter Magazine*, and *Digital Artist Magazine*

Gallery

"Maxwell Poisonvein."

LA MUERTE ROSA
(The Pink Death)

"The Pink Death."

"William Shakespaw."

ILLUSTRATION

"Sheep in Wolf's Clothing."

"Cosmos."

MIKE THOMPSON

About the Artist

I began my professional career as both a designer and an illustrator after graduating in 1990 from the University of Maryland with a degree in graphic arts. Fashion designer/CCO Marc Ecko personally recruited me to head his company's T-shirt department in 1997. In 2002, my artwork was prominently integrated into Ecko's advertising campaign; this set the brand apart from its competitors and gained the interest of several recording artists. My portraits of personalities such as Jay-Z, Kanye West, and the Roots have solidified me as a major presence in the urban art world.

In 2003, I made the decision to leave Ecko Unlimited and work for myself. Since forming Mike T Artworks, LLC, I have been featured in two separate national media campaigns for Coca-Cola and Infiniti Motors. I have created paintings for multiple magazines as well as book and video game covers. Numerous international publications have run features on my work and techniques.

Over the past few years, I have been extremely busy bringing my unique illustrative style to several major companies. I have painted Ken Griffey, Jr., for Nike, Kid Rock for Atlantic Records, and Heath Ledger for Warner Bros. In 2009, the Weinstein Company showcased my work for the Dimension Films movie *Youth in Revolt*. Recently I developed a relationship with Hasbro and am creating a series of dynamic illustrations for its GI Joe figure line.

I am represented exclusively, worldwide, by the David Goldman Agency in New York City.

Artist's Statement

When I take on a new illustration, my prime goal is to top each preceding work—it must be more interesting, dynamic, and skillfully rendered than my previous paintings. By maintaining that approach, I don't become too comfortable. To me, being one's own worst critic can only make you a better artist.

MIKE THOMPSON

Studio

    Software: Snow Leopard, Painter, Photoshop

    Hardware: Mac Pro 2.66 Quad-Core Intel, Cinema HD Display, Wacom Intuos 4

Contact

    Mike Thompson ▪ Mike T Artworks ▪ Maryland, USA ▪ thatguy@miketartworks.com ▪ http://www.miketartworks.com

"Dilla."

Influences

I have many inspirations and influences. If we are talking about art, I am drawn to realism and portraiture first. Masters such as Michelangelo and da Vinci to contemporaries such as Jason Seiler and Sebastian Krüger have directly influenced my career. However, like many artists, I find inspiration all around me. I am just as moved to create by watching *The Matrix* or playing an epic video game as I am by a beautifully rendered painting.

Techniques

Step-by-Step Tutorial: "First Sunday" Movie Poster

The painting I will be describing was commissioned as part of a pitch for a movie titled *First Sunday*. This Screen Gems film stars Ice Cube, Tracy Morgan, and Katt Williams. The agency wanted to persuade the studio to use an illustrated poster for this film rather than a photographed one-sheet. After reading the description, I thought that painting this piece in the style of the 1970s era black exploitation film posters would work nicely. What I find so appealing about this genre of posters is that most of them were hand painted, and they gave the viewers all the best parts of the film at a glance. With that in mind, I was inspired to begin my painting.

1. The studio provided me with some excellent photos from the set. They allow me to get a real sense of the movie without seeing it. As an illustrator, I am rarely given this quality of reference material, so I am fairly happy at this point. I go through all the images and select the ones I feel tell the story. See Figure 14.1.

Figure 14.1   Select reference photos to work from.

2. I start this piece as I always do, by quickly sketching out a few roughs for the client. Because Cube, Tracy, and Katt are the main characters, the art director agrees that this composition works best. See Figure 14.2.

Figure 14.2 Rough sketch is approved.

3. Using the photos I selected earlier, I begin my drawing. Because this image will just be presented as a comp, I set up a new page in Painter with dimensions of about 10 inches × 12 inches at 200dpi. I select the basic paper and a modified pencil, create a new layer, and start to draw. Faces are always my starting point because I find them most interesting. Also, getting the portraits out of the way early gives me confidence that the rest of the piece will work. I am using the Erasers, Eraser, and my pencil size is set to 30, as is my opacity. See Figure 14.3.

NOTE

I really admire artists who can quickly do a gesture drawing and then figure out the specifics as they paint. Unfortunately, I am not one of those guys. One thing I've learned over the years is that I can save a lot of time in my painting by working out all my "issues" in the line drawing. I spend a lot of time making sure my clean pencils are close to how the final illustration will look. I even lightly draw in the lines where I'll place my highlights and shadows. By the time I actually start to paint, I have created a "paint-by-numbers" minus the numbers.

Figure 14.3 Draw the faces first.

223

4. Once I am happy with the main figures, I move on to the rest of the composition. I pay close attention to my original sketch and vary the size of the secondary characters. It is important that I maintain compositional harmony for this poster to work. The last addition of the movie logo ties the image together nicely. See Figure 14.4.

Figure 14.4   Develop a strong composition.

5. Next, I click the name of my layer, change it to Pencils, and check the Preserve Transparency box. Selecting my entire canvas, I fill my line drawing with a brown color from the Picker. I then set Blend mode to Multiply and drop Opacity to 60 percent. Finally, I fill the canvas layer with a bright orange base color. At this point, I am happy with the line and save my document as a PSD file. See Figure 14.5.

Figure 14.5   Adding base colors.

6. To keep my illustration warm, I select a bright yellow to work over the horizon. This painting needs to have a 70s feel, so I am mindful not to work too tightly. Using the Artist Oils and Oil Pastels, I sparingly build up my light areas. I use the Just Add Water blender to soften my transitions and create a wash for the background. Finally, I switch to white and paint out my negative areas. See Figure 14.6.

> **TIP**
>
> This subtractive technique is not the way I normally work. However, allowing some of the ground color to show through the white paint helps give my illustration the "vintage" look I want.

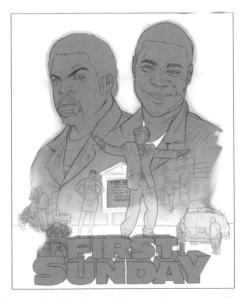

Figure 14.6 Use Just Add Water to soften color transitions.

7. Next, I create a third layer and place it between the canvas and line layers. This layer is labeled Color and is where I begin blocking in my flesh tones. In Figure 14.7, I lay down daubs of color near my subject using colors from my mixing pad. Now I can use the Eyedropper to select these colors, which saves time.

Figure 14.7 Place paints on the canvas to save time.

> **TIP**
>
> I have set the Rocker button on my Wacom pen, so clicking forward changes my brush to the Eyedropper, and clicking back and dragging on the canvas scales the size of my brush.

8. At this point, I don't really care about the likenesses; I just want to get the colors and tones on the faces. I take a break from Ice Cube and begin to work in the lighter tones of Tracy's face. When I am finished blocking in my colors, the transitions are pretty harsh, but I'll worry about that later. See Figure 14.8.

> **NOTE**
>
> My general rule is not to be too heavy handed with the Blender. I don't want this painting to look airbrushed, and I definitely don't want it to feel digital. Texture and stroke are important to me. Using the Blender at this stage isn't a big concern because I'll be painting over these areas.

Figure 14.8 Highlights are added to the skin tones.

9. I create a new layer above the pencil lines and name it Details. This layer is where I will refine my painting. I switch to my Just Add Water Blender and get to work on some of those hard transitions. See Figure 14.9.

Figure 14.9 Soften the edges of highlights.

10. I switch to a modified Scratchboard tool now. I have to give a huge shout-out to one of my favorite artists, Ryan Church, for his version of this tool. It is, without a doubt, my favorite Painter tool of all time! Remaining on the Details layer, I dial in their likenesses and begin adding detail to their coveralls and Katt's clothes. See Figure 14.10.

Figure 14.10 Begin working in details.

Figure 14.11 Use the Scratchboard tool for small details.

> **TIP**
>
> Taking frequent breaks can really help you catch problems with your work. Also, don't forget to save frequently—you never know when your machine might crash!

> **TIP**
>
> Rather than taking a chance painting over something I like, I add a new layer. When I am satisfied, I collapse the layers above my pencils, create another, and continue painting. Working this way allows me to make as many tweaks as I need, without letting the size of the file get too large.

11. More work on Katt Williams—this is where the Scratchboard tool really comes in handy. Pressing lightly on the stylus gives a thin, crisp line, so it is perfect for small details like these. See Figure 14.11.

12. Taking a break from Ice Cube has allowed me to see that he needs a lot of work! I soften the lines above and below Cube's eyes and get rid of the highlights on his pupils. Now he looks more like the rapper-turned-actor and not a crazed prisoner of war. See Figure 14.12.

ILLUSTRATION

Figure 14.12 Refining details in the face.

13. I am almost done now, so I shift my focus to the background and paint in the vignettes. These areas are fairly small, so a little detail goes a long way. Again, I allow areas of the canvas to integrate into these scenes (see Figure 14.13). While painting, I constantly refer to my photos and original reference poster for direction.

Figure 14.13 Finish the background details.

14. As you can see from the finished piece in Figure 14.14, I made a few changes. The advertising agency decided that it wanted a different expression for Tracy and wanted Katt to be larger with a new head. Once I finished the painting, I dropped all the layers to canvas, raised the resolution to 300dpi, and presented it to the client. Ultimately, the movie studio decided to go with a photograph of the three principal actors. However, the good news is, the director of *First Sunday* recently gave me a call personally. He let me know he wished the studio had gone with my illustration. He also sent me a photo of my painting, which he has framed and hanging in his office.

Figure 14.14 "First Sunday" final image.

ILLUSTRATION

Insights

The Creative Process

Each day I spend at least half an hour scouring the Internet for new images. I've built an extensive library of thousands of photos and pieces of art using a "5-second rule." Because I click through so many pictures so quickly, I've decided that anything that can keep me from pressing the Next button for at least 5 seconds is saved. That library serves as inspiration for lighting, gesture, mood, and so on. My actual workflow when creating a new painting is fairly common: sketches, clean line drawing, painting, and then obsessing.

I use Painter 11 every day. It has become essential to my workflow. I tend to do the bulk of my work in Painter and then use Photoshop for color correction and tweaks. Moving between applications has become pretty seamless.

Favorite Features

I love the natural media that Painter offers. The materials give such a convincing impression of their "real-life" counterparts that it is hard to tell the difference. Unlike other applications, I can approach a painting the same way I would traditionally. I also like having the ability to mix media that either doesn't work or is extremely difficult to do in real life. This allows me to express my creativity without limitations. I use the Real Media tools to create paintings for clients who want the quick turn-around time of digital but the look of traditional illustration.

Customizable Tools

I have a small set of custom tools that I use to get the look of my paintings. I use a few modified Artist Oils Brushes and the Scratchboard tool, in addition to the stock Oil Pastel and Blender Brushes. Because I have become so reliant on these tools, I have placed them into custom tool palettes (see Figure 14.15). Over time, I have also created a mixer pad that I use for all my work (see Figure 14.16). Saving these UI elements has greatly streamlined my daily workflow.

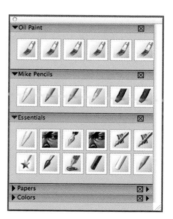
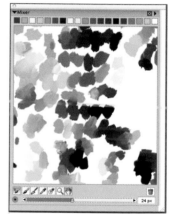

Figure 14.15 Custom tools.   **Figure 14.16** Mixer pad.

Timesaving Tips

One of the most valuable features of Painter is the ability to scale an image with minimal distortion. This allows me to work my piece at 100 percent of the reproduction size at 200dpi and then later scale it to 300dpi for printing. Working this way frees memory and enables me to move through a large project much quicker than working at full print resolution.

Finished Work

Most of the work I do is for magazine or book usage, so without a doubt the most important thing is proper color calibration/ reproduction. I've had pieces I spent countless hours working on totally ruined by a bad print job. Having an illustration print too light or too dark or seeing the colors shift can negate any pride I take in a job well done. That's another good thing about posting work online. An illustration can be shown to potential clients as intended, rather than shown as a bad tear sheet.

Q&A

When did you start using Painter?

I started using Painter about 3 years ago. I had been using Photoshop to paint for 12 years prior to that. Although I've owned every version of Painter since 5, I only really made the switch once Corel streamlined the interface. To be honest, I always knew it was a great application, but I found the user interface (UI) in earlier versions too intimidating to switch from Photoshop.

What do you wish someone had told you when you started?

When I first started with Painter, I was frustrated that it didn't behave exactly like Photoshop. I think I took the whole conversion process way too seriously. I had been working for so long using only two basic brushes in Photoshop that I felt overloaded when given all these new options in Painter. I wish someone had let me know to relax a little and just have fun.

Did you have previous experience in traditional media?

Yes. I began my artistic career as a traditional illustrator. I used acrylics on cold-press illustration board as well as airbrush on fabrics. Does the Bedazzler count?

Do you integrate your work in Painter with traditional artists' materials?

I have made prints that I later embellished with acrylics. I'd like to do more when I have some free time.

Has Painter helped you to define your own style?

One thing I hate about a lot of digital art is the "digital art" look. It's the look that is perfectly smooth and sterile with no sense of personality. I believe the biggest testimony to Painter is that viewers are usually surprised when I tell them I paint with my computer. The style I have developed over the years has evolved to feel more "hand made" using Painter.

What motivates you?

I am really motivated by all things creative, whether it is art, films, sculpture, or video games—anyone who takes his craft to the next level and makes me want to push myself to do better work.

Which artists do you admire?

As an illustrator, I've always had a great respect for Norman Rockwell. The way he captured everyday life around him so quickly and masterfully is still seldom matched. A hundred years from now someone will still be able to look at one of his paintings and tell exactly how the characters felt when he painted them.

The artist who really caused me to go into this profession was Ernie Barnes. Growing up, I wasn't taught about any successful artists who looked like me. Although I loved the art of the "classic painters," I couldn't relate to them. Like many other kids, I watched too much television and was introduced to Barnes's work while watching the show *Good Times*. His "Sugar Shack" painting featured during the credits was the most kinetic piece of art I had ever seen. Years later, when I learned more about his accomplishments, I knew this was the career for me.

How has the Internet influenced your art-making process?
The Internet has had a massive influence on my work. It has opened my eyes to the work of some outstanding artists I might not have had access to otherwise. It allows me to post works in progress for feedback, as well as finished art for promotion. I am also afforded the luxury of an extra day or two to finish a piece, because I no longer need to ship a disc to clients.

What advice do you have for artists working with Painter?
My advice would be to select a small set of tools that you can master rather than trying to learn everything at once. Once you are completely comfortable with them, shift your focus to other aspects of the program. As I said earlier, I used to be so put off by "everything" Painter had to offer that I didn't want to use it. I never felt like I had time to learn it all.

Resources

On the DVD
- Artist Gallery
- Mike T Videos
- Mike T Custom Brushes
- Mike T Custom Wallpapers

Links
- http://www.miketartworks.com
- http://www.thegnomonworkshop.com
- http://www.adigranov.net
- http://www.cgsociety.org
- http://sebastian-kruger-news.blogspot.com
- http://www.illustrationmundo.com/wp/
- http://www.aintitcoolnews.com
- http://twitter.com

MIKE THOMSON

Education

BA in graphic arts

Client List

Hasbro, Coca-Cola Company, Dimension Films, Atlantic Records, Warner Bros., Electronic Arts (EA), HBO, Infiniti Motors, Nike, Puma, Target, and T-Mobile

Awards and Career Highlights

Starred, along with my work, in a national Coca-Cola television commercial and was featured by Infiniti Motors for its "Infiniti in Black" national ad campaign. I've also been commissioned to paint several sport, entertainment, and musical artists.

Gallery

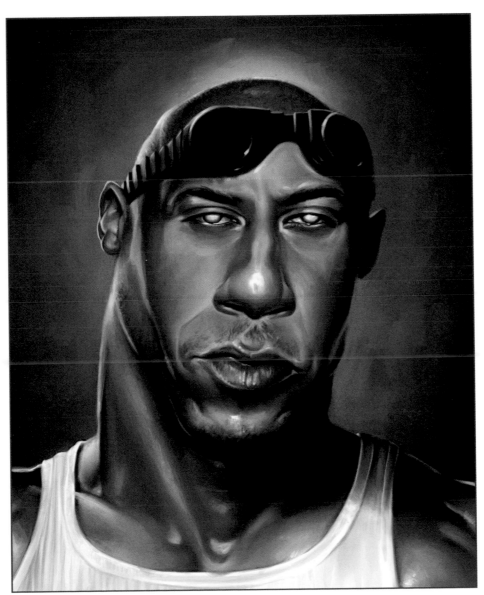

"Pitch Black."

ILLUSTRATION

"Lara."

"Chun Li."

MIKE THOMPSON

ILLUSTRATION

236

"Weekend@Bernie's."

MIKE THOMPSON

"Youth in Revolt."

DWAYNE VANCE

About the Artist

I graduated from Art Center College of Design with a BS degree in transportation design. I began my design career with Troy Lee Designs in Corona, California, as a designer of high-end motocross protective gear. I then became a senior designer for Mattel, Hot Wheels division. While at Hot Wheels, I designed and developed several cars and led teams for entire toy lines. I eventually returned to Troy Lee Designs. There, I continued to design cutting-edge motocross gear, including the SE2 helmet and other protective equipment. I now have my own company, Future Elements—High Energy Art and Design. I also have my own line of prints based on hot rod and muscle car art.

Artist's Statement

I love motion and speed. When you represent those well, they pull the viewer into your piece because they evoke an emotion.

Influences

I really feel that I got into design and art because of *Star Wars*. As a young kid, I was inspired to create things that didn't exist; I could create a whole new world that had never been explored. Still to this day, I love to draw robots and spaceships. I love manmade vehicles and the mechanics behind them. I am enamored with World War II just because of the fact the vehicles were so raw back then—but they functioned, and humans figured out how to make them work well. Science fiction and historical vehicles inspire me, and I like to bring them together, just like *Star Wars* was done. Some of my other influences are graffiti, anime, cartoons, graphic design, and nature.

DWAYNE VANCE

Studio

 Software: Painter, Photoshop, Illustrator, ArtRage, Alchemy

 Hardware: Intel Core i7, Wacom Cintiq 21UX

Contact

 Dwayne Vance ■ Future Elements ■ California, USA ■ dwayne@futureelements.net ■ http://www.futureelements.net ■ http://www.mastersofchickenscratch.com

"Hurryin' Back."

Techniques

Step-by-Step Tutorial: Hot Rod Vignette

I am going to be showing how I create a monotone sketch of one of my hot rod designs. It looks great as a quick presentation sketch and can be created quickly. I use a method called *vignetting*. It is a technique that creates a focal point toward the front and fades it out in the back. What I do to achieve this effect is render the front area and leave it as a sketch toward the back. This gives it more of a hand-drawn look and a focal point that takes one's eye from the front to back.

1. I start with some reference photos from car shows I have been to. In the photo in Figure 15.1, I am referencing a 1932 Ford, so I want to draw a '32 Ford—three-window version. I start by sketching the wheels to get my proportions, and then I rough out the beginnings of my sketch.

Figure 15.1   Rough draft from reference photos.

2. Figure 15.2 shows the rough sketch with all my proportions right. I use it as an underlay to make a nice clean sketch.

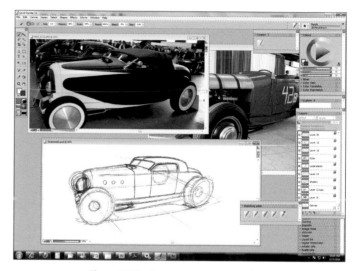

Figure 15.2   Focus on correct proportions.

3. In Figure 15.3, I fade the image back using the Opacity setting in the Layers palette. Then I create a new layer on top of the rough sketch to draw my clean drawing on.

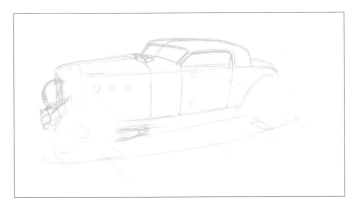

Figure 15.3   Create a clean sketch in a new layer.

4. I use a Wacom Cintiq to draw all my images so I can draw directly on the monitor. In Figure 15.4, I use my sweeps and French curves to clean up my lines on the car body. I do this by placing the templates directly on the monitor.

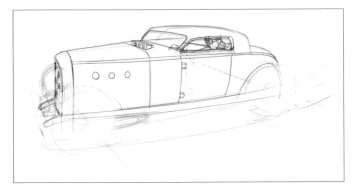

Figure 15.4   Use drafting templates to clean up line work.

5. In Figure 15.5, I lay in my cleaned-up wheels. Just as in the step before, I use ellipse guides and place them directly on the monitor to clean up the wheels.

Figure 15.5   Use ellipse guides to draw wheels.

6. To give my digital drawing a hand-drawn look, I use a gray marker to draw several strokes on a piece of paper. Next, I scan and import the image into Painter. See Figure 15.6.

Figure 15.6   Hand-draw marks on paper.

TIP

Create a small custom brush palette for yourself by dragging the brush you want onto the canvas. You can continue to add brushes to the custom palette after it has been created.

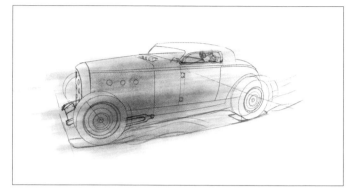

Figure 15.8   Scanned marks behind rough sketch.

7. In Figure 15.7, I change the color of the scanned marker strokes by using Effect, Tonal Control, Adjust Colors. I can change this to any color I would like; for this sketch, I decide I want it in the brown tones.

Figure 15.7   Adjust color of scanned marker lines.

8. I place my brown marker strokes behind the cleaned up sketch to give it some instant texture. I also remove the rough sketch from underneath the clean sketch by turning off the layer; this way I still have my original sketch for reference. See Figure 15.8.

9. In Figure 15.9, I lay in a ground shadow underneath the car. The brush I use for this is the Chalk Brush, with a custom setting for Square Chalk.

Figure 15.9   Add shadow underneath car.

10. I move on to defining other parts of the car. In Figure 15.10, I fill in the areas of the car body to bring out the form. I am still using the Square Chalk Brush and an Eraser Brush to create the forms.

Figure 15.10   Give form to the car body.

11. In Figure 15.11, I add some highlights to the metal by using the F-X, Glow Brush. This brush is similar to color dodge: just keep laying color until it becomes brighter and gives a metallic look to the car body.

Figure 15.11   Add metallic highlights with Glow Brush.

12. In Figure 15.12, I start adding some details and finishing touches.

Figure 15.12   Add details to the car.

13. I decide to add all the body cut lines using a lighter color and the F-X, Glow Brush again. Figure 15.13 shows the completed sketch with dust coming up from the wheels.

Figure 15.13   "Runnin' Flat 2," final image.

Step-by-Step Tutorial: Custom Cloud Brush

In the next few steps, I show you how to create the Custom Cloud Brush I used to create the dust. You can add it to your Painter arsenal.

1. I begin by using the Pattern Selector menu in the Patterns palette (or use Ctrl/Cmd+9 to bring up the menu) and select Make Fractal Pattern. Then I decide which adjustments I prefer. See Figure 15.14.

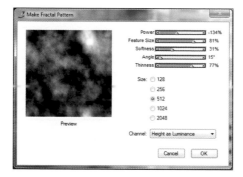

Figure 15.14   Select Make Fractal Pattern.

2. After I finish creating the fractal pattern, I click OK, and the pattern is created in a new window. Next, I select Effects, Tonal Control, Negative. This takes some of the black out of the fractal and makes a better brush. See Figure 15.15.

3. I use the Oval Selection tool and create a small circle in the middle of the fractal. Then I choose Select, Feather and set it to 50 pixels. See Figure 15.16. After that, I choose Select, Invert Selection, and click Backspace/Delete to delete the remaining fractal.

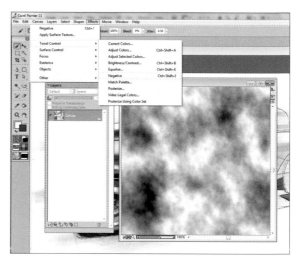

Figure 15.15   Select Effects, Tonal Control, Negative.

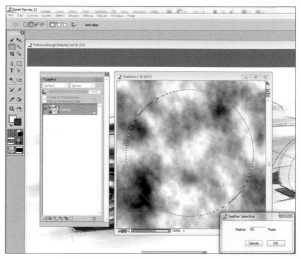

Figure 15.16   Feather and Invert Fractal.

4. Figure 15.17 shows what I am left with after the previous steps.

Figure 15.17   Circular fractal pattern.

5. I go to the Sponges Brush palette and select Dense Sponge. Then I use the Rectangular Selection tool and select the fractal I just created. I go to the upper-right corner and select the black arrow next to the brush descriptions, and I click on Capture Dab. See Figure 15.18.

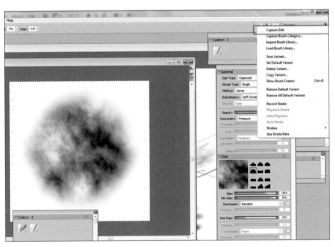

Figure 15.18   Select Capture Dab.

6. In Figure 15.19, I go back to the same black arrow in the upper-right corner and select Save Variant. I choose a name for my new brush. Then I go into the Sponges Brush palette and find the sponge brush that I just created. Now I am ready to use it.

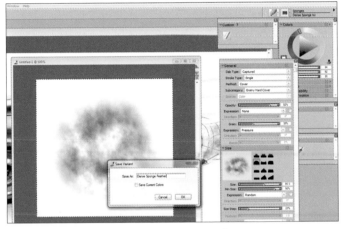

Figure 15.19   Save Variant and name.

7. Now I can use the new brush and create different brushes from it. In Figure 15.20, I use the Brush Controls palette to change different settings and create new brushstrokes. This is the outcome of the brush.

NOTE

Just have fun with Painter and figure out the best way for *you* to use the software. I use many techniques and play around a lot to figure stuff out. Give yourself some time to play, and don't worry about your art.

Figure 15.20 Change settings for different strokes.

Insights

The Creative Process

I have several creative processes. My favorite type is the sketch. I love the raw, first part of a design process when I'm trying to figure out my composition or design. Then I love adding the color through markers, paint, or digital paint.

Favorite Features

My favorite feature in Painter is the fact that I can make stuff look hand drawn. It doesn't have that digital look to it if I control the tools the right way. I probably use the pencils the most because I use Painter a lot for my initial sketch phase. I have created a variety of colored pencils, and they work great. I love that an image builds up color as I draw over the same lines. It really creates a colored-pencil look.

Customizable Tools

I don't create many crazy custom brushes. I tend to stick with what Painter gives me. But I *have* created a few custom colored pencils that I use a lot.

Timesaving Tips

I do a lot of industrial design work, and I use a Wacom Cintiq tablet along with Painter. To save time, I use my traditional ellipse guides and sweeps (drafting templates) and place them right onto the monitor to sweep my lines.

TIP

Create separate palettes for yourself with your favorite brushes. When I am working, I only open the palettes as I need them so they don't clutter my workspace. I give them separate names: sketch palette, paint palette, marker palette, and so on.

Finished Work

I display my finished work on gallery-wrapped canvases most of the time. At that point, I go back over my work with acrylic paint to put some texture back into it. I have also done a series of prints on different metals—from copper to aluminum. The printed works are displayed at different shows I attend and galleries throughout the world. The most important thing I consider when having work printed is using a company that knows how to produce high-quality gallery prints. A good company knows about the archival process—and that can make my prints last for 300 years plus. When I sell a high-end print, I want whoever buys it to feel she has purchased something special.

Q&A

When did you start using Painter?

I started using Painter during version 6, and I stuck with that version for a long time, possibly until Painter 9, and then I upgraded. Now I get to help with new versions of the program and give feedback to the developers.

What do you wish someone had told you when you started?

I wish someone had told me to start small. My advice to others is to just have fun and start with a few brushes; it's not necessary to learn what every brush does. When I work traditionally, I have only a few tools: a pencil, an eraser, maybe a few marker pens...not much. I try to think the same way digitally. An artist doesn't own every kind of medium, brush, paper, and canvas.

Did you have previous experience in traditional media?

Yes, my main background is in traditional art media. In school, I used a lot of pencils, markers, chalk, and occasionally gouache.

Do you integrate your work in Painter with traditional artists' materials?

Yes, I do, and a lot of times I create pieces. I can work digitally and play with color palettes, compositions, and so on. Then I can have my image printed and go back over it with traditional materials. A lot of times I rough out a sketch in Painter, print it and go over it with pencil, scan it back in, and finish it digitally. Like I said before, Painter is just another tool for an artist.

Has Painter helped you define your own style?

Painter has really made me a quick designer. What used to take me three or four hours to draw by hand, I can do with Painter in about two hours.

How does Painter fit into your creative process and workflow?

Painter works great into my workflow because it works just like a real pencil, and I still love the look of a hand-drawn sketch. When I work digitally, I can work a lot faster, have an unlimited color palette with no major cleanup, and have an unlimited number of Undos. Some might argue that working digitally is cheating because of that fact, but the computer is just another tool in an artist's palette.

What motivates you?

My main motivation for my work is a passion to create things that don't exist or could not be created by a photograph. I still draw things that I would have thought of as a child, and it takes me into a new world or a world with different technology.

How has the Internet influenced your art-making process?

The Internet has really influenced my art because I can see so many different techniques that other artists use and then adapt them to my own style. I can constantly learn stuff, and mostly for free. Sometime I have to pay for the high-end stuff, but the cost really isn't much when I am getting such a great education from it.

Which artists do you admire?

My favorite artist is God. He truly created an amazing universe to be inspired by. I also have a huge list of entertainment artists I like: Craig Mullins, Scott Robertson, and the guys at Steambot Studios. I also love classical painters, such as Édouard Manet, and others from the Impressionist period. I love to see brushstrokes.

DWAYNE VANCE

247

What advice do you have for artists working with Painter?

If you're just starting out with Painter, take some time and play with it. Get used to some of the functions and the different brushes. Don't feel that you have to use every brush it offers—find how you would normally work, either by hand or digitally, and start with a small palette of brushes. When I started using Painter, I made a custom palette for myself that consisted of two pencils and an eraser. As I got comfortable with using that and incorporated it more and more into my workflow, I started expanding. One flaw in Painter is that it feels overwhelming at first when you realize there are so many brushes. So start with a few and just play. Don't worry about making a masterpiece at first—you will grow after a while.

Resources

On the DVD

- Artist Gallery

Links

- http://www.futureelements.net
- http://www.mastersofchickenscratch.com
- http://www.google.com
- http://www.conceptart.org
- http://flaptraps.blogspot.com
- http://oldpainting.blogspot.com
- http://gurneyjourney.blogspot.com
- http://www.cardesignnews.com/site/home
- http://parkablogs.com
- http://www.idsketching.com

DWAYNE VANCE

Education

Art Center College of Design—BS in transportation design

Client List

Mattel—Hot Wheels, Batman, and entertainment divisions; Hasbro—Transformers and Star Wars division; Texaco; Oakley; Warner Bros; Mazda; Chumba Racing; Upper Deck; BlackStar Paintball; Arctic Cat Snowmobiles; Corel Painter; Jada Toys; Fly Racing; Troy Lee Designs; Flying Lizard Racing; EA Games; Activision; DC Comics; and a few others…

Awards and Career Highlights

Artwork displayed in Peterson Automobile Museum in the Hot Wheels Display. Have been published in several magazines and books, including *Imagine FX*; *Corel Painter Official* magazine; and *Hot Wheels: 35 Years of Speed, Power, Performance, and Attitude*

Gallery

"Snow Drift."

CONCEPT DESIGN

"Shoe Box."

"Runnin' Flat 1."

CONCEPT DESIGN

"Salt Flat Car."

"Belly Tanker."

CONCEPT DESIGN

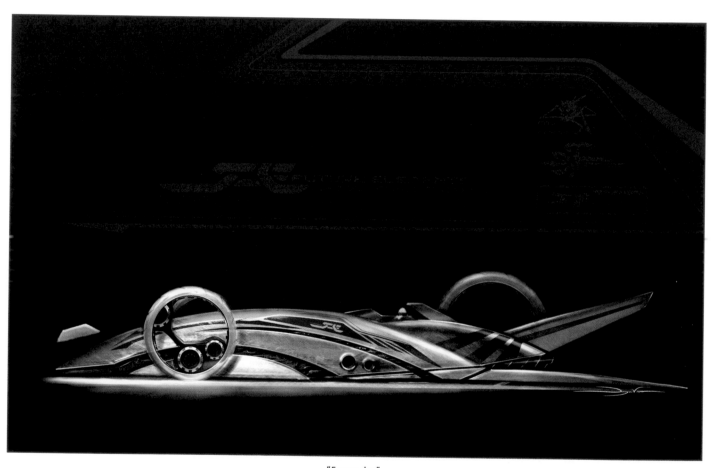

"Facepeeler."

"Mercy Striker."

"Protector of the Faith."

CONCEPT DESIGN

"Future Muscle."

"Fury of the Warhawk."

JOHN DERRY

About the Artist

I am a pioneer of digital painting and one of the original authors of Corel Painter. Since 1985, I have leveraged my background in drawing and painting to advance the look and experience of traditional art-making tools on the computer. I have a master's degree in painting from Cranbrook Academy of Art, am a practicing artist and photographer, and have two U.S. patents relating to expressive digital mark-making. Adobe recently designated me as a *Photoshop Painting Pioneer.* I teach digital painting workshops internationally and hold a photographic craftsman degree from Professional Photographers of America. I am a lynda.com author specializing in digital painting titles.

Artist's Statement

I am passionate about any tool I can use as a means of personal expression—particularly mark-making tools. The computer has spawned highly malleable mark-making tools that can both mimic their traditional counterparts as well as enable unconventional through-the-looking-glass visions. I use a variety of digital tools to blend media like painting and photography.

Influences

My influences include abstract expressionism, twentieth century illustration, music, popular entertainment media, daily observations, and life.

JOHN DERRY

Studio

    Software: Painter, Photoshop

    Hardware: MacBook Pro, Apple Cinema Display, Wacom Intuos 4 with Art Pen, Canon 5D and G10 cameras, Monaco Optix monitor calibrator, Epson 2200 and 7600 ink-jet printers with archival ink

Contact

    John Derry ■ Nebraska, USA ■ derry@pixlart.com ■ http://www.pixlart.com

"Circular Chicago."

Techniques

Step-by-Step Tutorial: "Chicago in the Round"

When I went photographically digital, a world of possibilities became ripe for exploration. I had always been interested in panoramas, but the technique required specialized equipment. In the digital realm, stitched panoramic imagery became doable. My panoramas eventually became the source for my next step: circular panoramas.

1. The basis for my circular panoramic technique begins with a traditional, horizontally oriented, stitched digital panorama. The primary tool that makes the circular technique possible is Painter's Pattern Pen. The Pattern Pen is a tool that Mark Zimmer and I created during the development of Corel Painter 6. This specialized brush segments the original imagery and mates it to a warpable mesh that acts as the stroke emerging from the Pattern Pen. The Pattern Pen is pressure sensitive—if desired—enabling dynamically changing width, based on the user's pen pressure when used in concert with a Wacom Pen (essential for getting the full expressibility of Painter). See Figure 16.1.

2. Mark and I had already developed a seamless pattern-making tool that enables the user to define any selected area as a pattern tile. This tile can then be offset by any amount within the image window. With this capability, the user can use any of Painter's formidable brush libraries to create and "seam" together image elements. The Pattern Pen relies on horizontally oriented, seamless patterns as the "paint" that the pen dispenses. Additionally, patterns can have a mask, which enables irregular elements to be used. Each sample in Figure 16.2 was drawn on individual layers. This setup opens a range of possibilities in concert with seamless patterns.

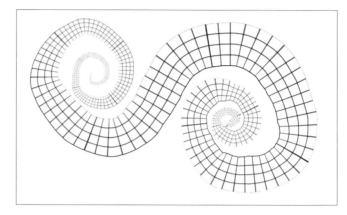

Figure 16.1 Pattern Pen grid path.

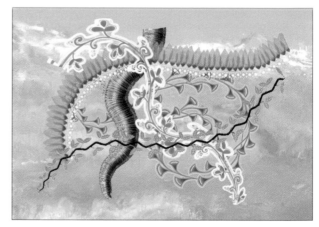

Figure 16.2 Decorative pens.

3. When I began creating digital "panos," it occurred to me that a horizontal panorama could be easily pressed into service as a Pattern Pen element. This led to developing a technique to conform the Pattern Pen's "paint" to a circle. Like Photoshop, Painter conveniently has a "Stroke Selection" option. All that remained was to experiment with the Pattern Pen's brush size and the circular selection's diameter to arrive at the desired result. Figure 16.3 shows my original panoramic photograph. This was shot during a Chicago architectural tour from the boat while it was a bit offshore.

Figure 16.4   Custom-created Chicago Pattern Pen.

Figure 16.3   Original Chicago panoramic photograph.

4. Note in Figure 16.5 the circular selection at the midway point of the stroked Pattern Pen panorama element. This is not an automatic process because Painter's combination of Pattern Pen, Brush Size, and circular selection diameter size used to perform this technique do not "know" about one another. It is instead an "experimentive" manual process that requires a bit of trial and error to achieve the desired result. But the result definitely makes it worth the effort!

Figure 16.5   Stroked Pattern Pen with circular selection.

5. You'll notice that the Pattern Pen-stroked circular selection shown in Figure 16.5 does not have a seamless mating of the ends of the stroke. This is another manual operation that must be performed as a retouching exercise. Each resulting circular panorama that I've created using this technique needs to be manually retouched to create the illusion of continuity. However, there is always enough source material available in both the resulting circular panorama as well as the original horizontal source pano to construct a convincing illusion.

6. Because these circular panos use high-resolution horizontal source panoramic photos, the resulting image is quite high resolution. The only limit is the Pattern Pen's brush width. Painter does have an upper limit of 1500 pixels for its brush width. Considering that the center of a circular pano is sky and can be blended to hide a "donut hole," a resulting image can easily be 3500–4000 pixels across. And then various interpolative techniques can increase that size for large-format output.

7. Another consideration is the treatment of the outer edge of the resulting circular image. Figure 16.6 shows a variation on the pano—shot at Point Lobos State Reserve outside of Carmel, California—using a radial blur technique to create an "aura" surrounding the circular panorama. This adds some additional "punch" to the original. If you look closely, you'll find that there is a person in this image. The individual is located between the 2 and 3 o'clock positions, standing at the top of the cliff (toward the center of the image). He is visible against the dark tree-shadowed background.

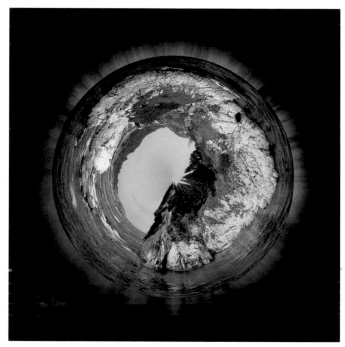

Figure 16.6 Blur the outside edge to produce an aura.

8. Another extension of this technique I've evolved is to play with the vertical orientation of the source image. As shown in Figure 16.7, depending on which way the vertical image axis is oriented, the sky can be wrapped either inward or outward.

9. For my "Circular Chicago" image, shown in Figure 16.8, I have taken Pattern Pen-originated panoramas and nested them, one inside the other, to create a mirrored effect. This "double pano" variant takes a bit more planning and trial-and-error to end up with the desired result, but, as I mentioned earlier, it is generally well worth the effort. Plus, I don't know of any other way to do it!

Figure 16.8   "Circular Chicago" final image.

Figure 16.7   Differing axis orientations to consider.

Insights

The Creative Process

Generally, I initially have a mental image or story. Sometimes I am struck by a unique juxtaposition of visual elements. I build an image in my mind's eye and then begin to construct the imagery using digital tools. At some point in the process, the image begins to take on a life of its own. I enjoy allowing mistakes and accidents to be incorporated into the piece. Most often, the result is somewhat different from the original concept.

Favorite Features

The Image Hose is great for quickly creating complexity in images that would otherwise be time consuming.

Customizable Tools

I custom-build most of my brushes to suit my expression. I create custom panels to organize my content for quick access.

Timesaving Tips

I create custom palettes to quickly retrieve oft-used tools and content. I also customize keyboard shortcuts to match Photoshop-applicable functions, which makes it easier to move between Painter and Photoshop. Finally, I save multiple iterations of an image in development, because the crash monster can appear unexpectedly.

Finished Work

Finished images are printed on archival Fine Art paper under glass or on a display. The most important things I consider are careful quality control for printed works to maintain consistent results and color management for Web-viewed imagery to maintain correct color and tone.

Q&A

When did you start using Painter?

I have using Painter since before version 1.0.

What do you wish someone had told you when you started?

I wish someone had told me it was going to be my primary focus for the next 19 years of my life.

Did you have previous experience in traditional media?

I have several years' experience in acrylic-based painting. I also have experience in serigraphy and hand lithography and have been a long-term photographer. I have worked in commercial print design and production—both analog and digital.

Do you integrate your work in Painter with traditional artists' materials?

I'm currently embellishing prints of paper with pastel pencils. I have a great desire to go "full circle" and begin mixing digitally created imagery with traditional painting techniques. Hopefully that will happen soon.

How does Painter fit into your creative process and workflow?

I have recently started using Photoshop CS5 for more painting activities, but Photoshop always occupies the initial (photo correction) and final stages (color and tonal refinement, output) of an image, whereas Painter (and now Photoshop) are in the middle for expressive mark-making activities.

Has Painter helped you define your own style?

It has enabled greater ability to change and evolve my artistic expression.

What motivates you?

I enjoy merging media like painting and photography. Through them, I enjoy communicating an emotion or story.

Which artists do you admire?

I admire twentieth century abstract expressionist Robert Rauschenberg. His work combined unconventional media (print/oil painting/silk screen/found objects) to create unique expressions.

How has the Internet influenced your art-making process?

The art community is now much more accessible. Ideas change and mutate quickly, which leads to greater idea evolution. There is much greater potential for feedback regarding one's visual statements.

What advice do you have for artists working with Painter?

Study traditional media. You don't have to necessarily experience it, but observing it will inform you of how imagery is put together.

Resources

On the DVD

- Artist Gallery

Links

- http://www.pixlart.com
- http://www.linesandcolors.com/
- http://bibliodyssey.blogspot.com/
- http://todaysinspiration.blogspot.com/
- http://virtualgouacheland.blogspot.com/
- http://bigstormpicture.blogspot.com/
- http://www.lynda.com/

JOHN DERRY

Education

BFA, MFA—painting and drawing

Awards and Career Highlights

Painter software author

FINE ART PHOTOGRAPHY

Gallery

"HHT Abstract."

"Equinox."

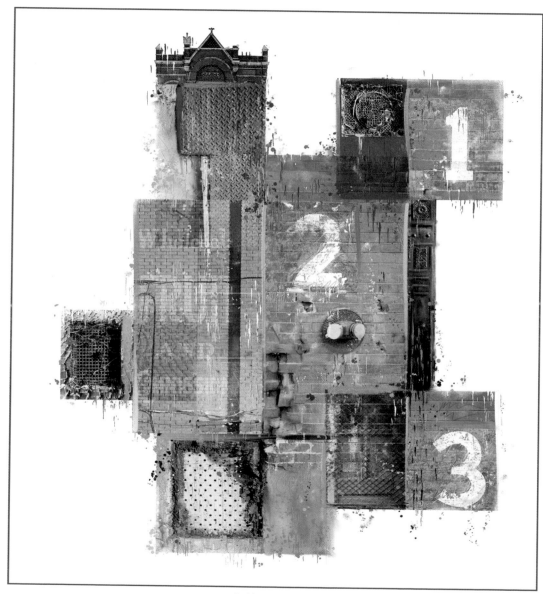

"Old Market Ghosts."

"Lone Belle."

"K.D. House."

Dundee Morn September 2009

"Dundee Morn."

JANE CONNER-ZISER

About the Artist

I am a photographer, digital artist, educator, and independent consultant. I have more than 25 years of experience, with 19 of them in digital imaging and evolving technologies. The techniques that I have developed for facial retouching and enhancement and portrait painting are widely emulated by photographers and digital artists worldwide. I was named as one of Canon's Explorers of Light in their Print Master program, am an Adobe Photoshop Expert, a Corel Painter Master, and a Craftsman Photographer with the Professional Photographers of America. I am also a past cochair for the Digital and Advanced Imaging Committee for the Professional Photographers of America. I have been referred to as one of the most versatile artists in the industry. My style, knowledge of my field, and easy, entertaining way of presenting challenging material have helped to make me one of the most significant educators in the industry today.

Artist's Statement

Art is one of the things that make life vibrant and meaningful. Creating art is like letting your spirit out of the house to wear clothes of emotion that others can see, hear, touch, feel, and taste. Art is important and powerful—sometimes it's like standing in the sun, and other times it's like cowering in the dark—always it is provoking.

I create art for two reasons. First, it's a product that I sell. For these pieces, I must channel my creativity into repeatable processes so my clients will receive a visually predictable finished piece that I can create in a frame of time that allows me to make a beautiful portrait and a beautiful profit. I focus on feeling the emotions I know my client wants to feel in the painting because that will express itself through my paint. I use music to take me there and hold my interest during the painting process, because most pieces, though pleasant enough, are not particularly challenging.

JANE CONNER-ZISER

Studio

Software: I use whatever! Painter, Photoshop, Nik Color Efex, Graphic Authority, Flaming Pear, LucisArt.

Hardware: Wacom tablet is my must have. And I prefer my Mac. I use both Canon and Epson printers.

Contact

Jane Conner-ziser ■ JanesMediaArt ■ Florida, USA ■ janecz@mac.com ■ http://www.janeconner-ziser.com

"When Doves Sigh."

When I create art for myself, it's different: I explore myself, stretch myself into places I haven't been before, and challenge myself to do things that are uncomfortable. I don't care if what I am doing would be considered "acceptable." Every personal piece has a lesson for me. Sometimes it's an easy one, and other times it can take months to learn—*and* open doors of depression or anxiety I never knew existed—and then I have *that* to deal with! So it's always a moving and learning experience for me, and I really don't care if other people like the results of my inner/outer experiments. Sometimes I don't like the results either! Ha!

I don't have a particular style of painting; I like variety and experimentation. I believe that every painting "calls" to be something, and I just have to be open to the discovery of it—before I sell the concept to a client. I believe my best paintings are a combination of education and discipline, plus spontaneous expression. It's a delicate balance that I don't always hit; some of my paintings are too structured, and others end up being something that doesn't resemble what I set out to achieve, but the ones in the middle are…just right.

Influences

I am inspired by everything, and I never know what will ignite my next burst of creativity—a photograph, music, nature, something I read someplace—I just kind of go with it.

My favorite painter is Rubens because of the robustness of his subjects. His work is sensual, generous, and fulfilling to experience. I just want to put my face on his canvases! I also love the work of Eduardo Costa, an unknown artist who owns a hair salon in Ormond Beach, Florida. His work is powerful, emotional, and bare.

Techniques

Step-by-Step Tutorial: Classic Oil-Style Portrait from Photography

This is a product technique for one of the portrait industry's top-selling portrait lines: the classic oil. It began in the "old days" when black-and-white photographs were printed on heavy paper (almost like cardboard) and charcoal was used to sharpen the areas that were blurry from extra long exposures. Before long, colors were also applied, and photographic artists began experimenting with a variety of traditional art media to take their images one step beyond the camera. By the time I came along, retouch artists were using liquid and wax-based photographic dyes, color pencils, pastels, gouache, oil paint, and acrylics.

Studio portrait lines have included photography: photography on mount board, photography on canvas board with brush-stroke embellishment; and top-of-the-line, the heavy oil. (The heavy oil was created by stripping the emulsion from a black-and-white photograph, adhering it to a canvas that was then stretched and hand-painted using traditional oil paints layered transparently over the photograph in some areas, and applied opaquely over others.) I always considered this last product to be the link between photography and painting, and I find it interesting that portrait photographers strive to make their photography look like paintings, whereas portrait painters work hard to get photographic likenesses of their subjects.

My process for creating this classic photo-oil painting with technology was developed from my experiments in creating digitally produced pieces that look like traditional mediums for classic portrait studio products. It is priced in the upper-middle section of portrait offerings, just under the most expensive portrait: a traditional painting from life. I consider Painter-created portraits to be a mid-priced hand-painted portraits because, by precomposing with photographs and using the photographic image for the under-painting, most of the busy-work is eliminated. Also, even when I take my time creating fantasy elements and adding artistic details, I can create a finished piece in a fraction of the time it would take if I started from scratch.

Classic oil portraits can be digitally painted faster and cleaner than ever before. I use a modified original color photograph as the under-painting, saving myself about 60 percent of the time it would take to create the colors from scratch. I precompose, color-adjust, enhance, size, and retouch in Photoshop and then paint in Painter—but this is just my personal preference and workflow I use for speed. I plan to have most classic oil paintings finished within 2 hours max.

1. I create my classic oil portrait starting with a photograph taken by Clay Blackmore of Rockville, Maryland, that was taken when he and I lectured together in Naples last spring. Clay and I make a lot of beautiful portraits together, and he is definitely one of my favorite photographer friends! The original capture is shown in Figure 17.1.

Figure 17.1 Original color portrait.

2. I see the portrait as a square so, using Photoshop, I crop and resize it for the 40-inch square canvas we plan to make. Notice in Figure 17.2 that I stretch the image on the right side to offset the body for better image balance. Because we shoot in RAW format, it is easy for me to bring out the vibrancy of the original colors without oversaturating them.

Figure 17.2 Adjust image size and composition in Photoshop.

NOTE

Many images are free to use, and others require a royalty payment. When I purchase images, I buy the low resolution, because I only use them for a sketch. When selecting images to collage into paintings, it is important to use those that have the same direction of light and adjust the colors to match the base image. Be particularly mindful of copyright—you don't want to steal another artist's work!

4. Using Photoshop, I flipped the bird image for the lighting to be consistent and to contain the viewer's eye within the painting (by having both heads facing each other). I color-adjusted the dove to have warmer neutrals, like those on the base image, plus I airbrushed some blue into the shadows on the woman's dress to repeat the cool shadows on the bird and to introduce additional color to the photograph. See Figure 17.4.

Figure 17.3 Add additional elements using Photoshop.

3. I like to add fantasy elements to my paintings, so it's not uncommon for me to photograph things I might want to use someday: clouds, the ocean, trees, furniture, and so on. I also use images I find on the Internet, like the dove shown in Figure 17.3.

FINE ART PHOTOGRAPHY

For adding color, it's common for me to use the Artists/ Impressionist Brush because it's fast and applies color randomly, as seen in Figure 17.5. Notice that when applying the accent colors, I curve the cool colors in a horseshoe around the body and add a bit of light to "crown" the subject's head. I create a round feminine shape for the mood of the piece and once again focus on holding the viewer's attention on the subject.

Figure 17.4 Use Photoshop to adjust color, light, and shadows.

> **TIP**
>
> Vertical linear direction is strong and steadfast, whereas horizontal linear direction is restful. Diagonal lines create motion; the stronger the diagonal lines are, the more aggressive the composition is.

5. At this point, the painting is created, from back to front, in three steps:

   1. Create the under-painting.
   2. Shape the focal point and important compositional elements.
   3. Add details and decorations.

The first step, using Painter, is to clone the image. From here I do two things: I continue to add or intensify colors in the background and clothing, and I begin to construct a custom palette for the piece. At this point I also choose the brush look I want. I like to vary my painting style so every painting can be unique, but I do have a few favorite brush styles.

Figure 17.5 Apply accent colors in Painter.

JANE CONNER-ZISER

6. I chose a free-spirited, almost dance-like quality for the mood of this painting. I want a heavy, greasy look to the paint. I select the Artists/Sargent Brush because I like the way the brush creates jagged edges and the way it resists thoroughly blending different colors. I make sure to add it to my custom palette. Then I create a clone from the image that the accent colors were added to and select Clone Color in the Colors palette. This allows for quick painting and less opportunity for overblending. While working on the background, I am free to paint over the dove. Later I will help it emerge from the background by adding details to the face and shoulders. I never try to protect parts of the original—I just paint over them later. I create this part of the painting while viewing the entire image. See Figure 17.6.

Figure 17.6   Clone colors and paint the background.

7. In the next steps, I blend the skin tones. I select the Airbrush/ Digital Airbrush and set it at 2 percent opacity. Then I add red to the parts of the skin where the shaded side moves into diffused highlight. See Figure 17.7. Sometimes I also add white to brighten specular reflections.

TIP

Music is a great partner to paint with. For this image, I listened to music that makes me feel light-spirited and dance-like, which puts me in the mood to express my feelings through the brushstrokes.

NOTE

Be conscious of where the paint is going to ensure that light and dark values are being placed in their correct locations. Anything that is applied should accentuate the focal point as well as the smooth development of the painting.

NOTE

Specular reflection is the mirror-like reflection of light from a surface—light from a single incoming direction is reflected into a single outgoing direction.

Figure 17.7 Add color to the skin tones.

Figure 17.8 Blend the skin tones.

8. After I've added the colors, I blend the skin with graceful circular motions (like applying shoe polish) using Blenders/ Grainy Water. For porcelain complexions, I set the opacity to 30 percent, or for more definite strokes, I might try 60 percent. This painting was blended at 40 percent with brush sizes that vary according to where I am working. I use small brushes in detailed areas, like around the nose and eyes, and larger brushes for the chest and arms. See Figure 17.8.

9. The dress is next. I want to find areas in which to create fantasy in the clothing; this way the painting will not look like a "smushed-around" photograph. In Figure 17.9, I painted the folds of fabric with specular-like highlights, diffused highlights, and shaded values that roll into each other. I start the flow of the gown by using Airbrush/Digital Airbrush to add color values and then move the existing gown, and my paint, around with the Distort/Pinch Brush.

NOTE

Most paintings develop from back to front, from large brushes to small brushes. The amount of time spent shaping the focal point and important compositional elements and adding details and decorations determines how much detail the result will have.

TIP

Fabric is more interesting when additional colors are added and the flow of the fabric contains both areas of sharp creases and areas of graceful ripples.

Figure 17.9 Create fantasy in the clothing.

Figure 17.10 Create folds in the fabric.

10. In Figure 17.10, I form the gown during the blending process. I can choose any blender variant, but because I am going for a smooth "floaty" look, I select the Blenders/Pointed Stump and use it at 100 percent opacity. I create the fabric by following separate folds of fabric from where they begin to the edges of the garment. I create sharp folds by working different values next to each other, and soft folds by brushing across the edges between different values. Flowing fabric is just a combination of light, medium, and dark values making interesting shapes. I try to create fantasy shapes and have fun!

11. I create the hair in two steps. I add color and shape using Palette Knives/Tiny Smeary Knife 5. In Figure 17.11, I select colors from the hair and make them lighter or brighter. I apply the highlights according to how the light might shine naturally on the shapes I am creating.

Figure 17.11 Add shapes and highlights to the hair.

FINE ART PHOTOGRAPHY

12. I then reshape the hair and blend it using Palette Knives/
Tiny Palette Knife 5 at 100 percent opacity. See Figure 17.12.

Figure 17.12 Blend highlights into the hair with Palette Knives.

Figure 17.13 Evaluate edges, contrast, color, and detail.

13. At this point the under-painting is finished, and it is time
to evaluate the work for edge development, overall contrast, color, and detail. I reselect the brushes I've used
before, now making the brush sizes smaller to refine the
edges between the background and the subject, add more
folds and details to the clothing and hair, and create more
depth where it's needed. See Figure 17.13.

14. In Figure 17.14, I create additional depth in the image by
lightly glazing over areas that I want to make darker using
the Digital Watercolor/Broad Water Brush. At this point,
I sometimes take the painting back into Photoshop and
brush in Screen and Multiply versions of the painting to
bring out highlights and shadows.

Figure 17.14 Create depth by glazing with additional color.

15. When the painting holds together well and the degree of detail gracefully decreases as the eye looks farther from the face, it's time for the final step: adding details and decorations. I usually apply details using Airbrush/Digital Airbrush at 10 percent opacity in a new layer over the painting. See Figure 17.15.

Figure 17.15 Create a new layer to apply details.

16. In Figure 17.16, I enhance the facial features, add details to the hair, create fabric detail in the cameo area of the portrait, and sparkle up the jewelry. I choose colors from the painting and enhance them in value and saturation in the Colors palette prior to applying them in the new layer. Then I adjust the layer opacity to make the detail additions more delicate and blend the new work into the painted layer by using a small Blender Brush—Grainy Water, Pointed Stump, and Smear are some of my usual choices.

TIP

When painting eyes, view both at the same time so you avoid making the subject look cross-eyed.

Figure 17.16 Enhance facial features and add details.

NOTE

The goal for this style of painting is to create a detailed, photo-realistic painting in the cameo area of the portrait (the head and chest area), plus all skin tones, and then gradually add fantasy and a heavier brush technique as you move away from the focal point. The background and clothing usually reflect full brush work—hence the name *heavy oil* (as opposed to a transparent hand-colored photo). Every artist develops her own look through her strokes, but the end product is consistent in detail development.

FINE ART PHOTOGRAPHY

17. Figure 17.17 shows the final painting prior to finishing.

Figure 17.17 The painted photograph.

18. When a full brush painting like this is finished, it's common to add a brushed texture prior to printing on bright white artist canvas.

I apply surface textures and sharpening to the image in final size and resolution. When I upsize the final painting to print larger than I like to work in Painter, I resize the image prior to applying the textures. I apply surface brushstrokes while viewing the painting at 100 percent (actual size).

I then choose Effects, Surface Control, Apply Surface Texture, Using Image Luminance. Amount and Shine can be adjusted to taste; I set them at 16 percent for Amount and 8 percent (half) for Shine. See Figure 17.18. In Figure 17.19, the surface textures are applied.

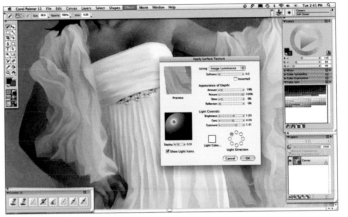

Figure 17.18 Using Image Luminance.

Figure 17.19 Surface texture applied to the final image.

19. After printing, I allow the image to dry for at least 24 hours and then seal it with a protective gloss or semigloss coating. This protects the surface and brings out a little bit more contrast and saturation. Once the protective coating is fully dry, I stretch the canvas. I might also apply additional surface embellishments at this point. See Figure 17.20.

Figure 17.20 "When Doves Sigh" final image.

Insights

The Creative Process

My creative process begins with an idea that has to sprout into a feeling. If it's for a client, as the previous image was, I usually begin with an interview with my potential subject. During the interview, I try to get a good feel for who the client is, what kinds of clothing are characteristic for her, what colors are appealing, and so on. I also watch her body language to learn how she moves and expresses herself. I make notes of which styles of painting she is most drawn to, and I begin thinking of her in that manner. Usually during the interview, I discover where and how the photography will happen. I try to book out a week or so to give myself time to absorb more of the client and see what other ideas may present themselves.

During the photography session, I follow what the client and I planned to do and then let the session go its own direction, where I continue using my "pro" camera (Canon 5D Mark II), or I pick up my pocket camera (Canon S90) and snap away. While editing the images, I usually notice a few that stand out as having great potential for paintings. I pull them aside to discuss with the client prior to creating the piece.

Other times I work with photography from other people, both fellow professionals and clients, when they have a favorite image. In these instances, I choose the image that makes the best painting and go from there. I try hard not to trap myself into having to struggle with an image that would be better left as photography. The image has to project a sense of motion, energy, and fantasy to be a WOW painting.

JANE CONNER-ZISER

When painting from photographs, the quality of the initial image is important. I'm a professional photographer, so I know lighting ratio, body positioning, perspective from camera lens, exposure—all the ingredients needed to create an artistic image through photography. I've been in the business for more than 30 years both as a photographer and artist and continue to study so I can continue to improve my work.

The painting process is simple. The first step is adding colors and creating a loose under-painting while viewing the full image onscreen. The second step is creating fantasy by adding additional colors, shapes, and values and beginning to develop the focal point areas by zooming in closer and using smaller brushes. The final step is adding details and decorations to the focal point(s). I expect to have most photo-paintings completed within 2–3 hours, though the three steps may be divided into separate painting sessions that may occur over a few days' time. Many times I like to get away from a painting and come back to it later with fresh eyes.

One of the most important things when painting from photographs is to deviate from the photograph whenever possible and create something that looks distinctively different from the original. Many people pride themselves on taking hours to blend every minute detail of the photograph, every leaf and every eyelash, but the end result looks like a photograph that perhaps had some airbrushing applied to it. In my experience, clients will usually say, "that's nice but I'll take the photo on canvas" because it's less expensive. I change the photograph through artistic image adjustments, color additions, enhancements, and by adding my own "pieces" and expressive brush-work.

Favorite Features

I use simple processes in Painter. For me it's all about the experience and application rather than the technology. I like the Smart Auto Painting feature for getting a quick start on the under-painting when working with complex backgrounds, but I always go back over it to add diversity and personal direction to the piece. I like the ability to make my own texture and special effects brushes, though I often delete them after the painting is complete. I try not to rely upon the same brush, the same texture, and the same boring way of applying things any more than I have to. I like the Digital Watercolor category for glazing.

Customizable Tools

I create most of my paintings using default brushes because I teach a lot of beginner painters, and they have enough to deal with just learning how the software works and figuring out how to move their hands. The magic is *not* in the brush; it's in the way it's moved. I discourage artists from becoming reliant upon a particular tool; it's too dependent, uncreative and confining—the opposite of what art should be. Painter's default brushes have been thoughtfully created by some of the best Painter artists in the world—and there's loads of them! That being said, I often make my own brushes for foliage, grass, rocks, and so on. I don't keep most of these custom brushes, because I prefer to build something unique for every piece. I also build custom palettes while I work and save a copy of those in the client's file in case there are edits. When the job is completed, I usually delete them.

Timesaving Tips

I precompose using cuts and pastes from (my) photographs and take advantage of Auto Painting on complex backgrounds.

FINE ART PHOTOGRAPHY

Finished Work

For my finished work, I want the image to be published with good value, color, and contrast and to look nice in the publication. I also want it to show in reputable places with visible artist credit, copyright, and contact information. I gallery-wrap or hand-stretch and frame oils. I matte and frame watercolors with clear glass.

Q&A

When did you start using Painter?

I started using Painter about 12 years ago. I used to do photo painting with oil paints on top of black-and-white photography. Once I realized the potential of technology, I was sold—until I realized that the software was a bit delicate on the 200+MB files that were typical in the photography industry at that time. Since then, the file sizes that photographers work with have gotten significantly smaller, and the software is a lot more sophisticated and fast. Now it's a pleasure to work with Painter!

What do you wish someone had told you when you started?

When I started using Painter for photo painting, I couldn't find anyone who was doing it, so I had to forge ahead on my own. Now there are so many educational opportunities that it's hard to pick the one that's just right! I would say to new artists to research the teachers you hear about, choose those whose work you admire and would strive to create yourself, make sure they have the knowledge and experience to teach you, and then go for it!

Did you have previous experience in traditional media?

I began receiving painting lessons when I was 7 years old and have continued to study art through private classes, public classes, books, and the Internet.

I started with pencil, charcoal, and chalk, and then I went to oils—which I still love. I have a classic and traditional art background. I never liked working with acrylics because they felt too opaque and dried too fast for me, though the modern acrylics are pretty amazing. I've always been a huge admirer of watercolors but never a good painter of them—until Painter. Now I can take all the time I need and go back over something a hundred times until I get just what I want!

How has it been for you to learn about using art tools in a digital setting?

I find it is easier to teach an artist how to use technology than teach a technician how to paint.

Do you integrate your work in Painter with traditional artists' materials?

Sometimes I start with Painter and finish with paint, or I use Painter as an enhancement to photography. It's versatile enough to play with in a variety of ways.

Has Painter helped you to define your own style?

It allows me to create anytime, anyplace, and anywhere, even when I know I won't have the time to finish before packing it up for a while. I get to create more without feeling pressed for time, and it makes it a lot more fun.

How does Painter fit into your creative process and workflow?

Painter is my mid-priced portrait line. It is priced higher than photography on canvas and lower than traditionally painted one-of-a-kind portraits.

What motivates you?

Money is always nice, but I would paint anyway because I love the experience of it; it makes me feel good. It's purely an emotional gratification.

How has the Internet influenced your art-making process?

I don't do a lot of art-making on the Internet, but I do a lot of product creation with my art—like purses, T-shirts, jewelry—I also market online. I would say that the Internet has given me the opportunity to be my own department store of creative and unique fine art pieces.

What advice do you have for artists working with Painter?

Relax, put on some music, and play. There's nothing you can do to ruin your piece; you can always erase or go back. And don't be too critical of your work—count the things you did well, along with the things you need to work on. Appreciate that every piece has a lesson for you. You'll know you're there when the piece looks terrible and you don't know what to do to fix it—that's when you rely upon what you know as far as value, contrast, color, detail, line, shape, perspective, focus, and so on to help you struggle through. After completing that phase, the lesson will have been learned. Let it go, and put the lesson to use on a new piece. Don't look back and mock your previous work; look back and smile at the beauty of where you were…and realize how you've grown.

Is there anything else you would like to say?

I love my Painter portraits! I believe it opens the world of fine art to a huge segment of society that might not have the money to purchase original paintings but appreciates first-generation images, hand-painted and hand-signed by the artist—*and* the ability to use custom-created art for other products like gift portraits, jewelry, stationery, clothing—okay, I'm a capitalist! Or, rather, I love to continue my education and exploration of the possibilities of art and technology! Thank you!

NOTE

I say that I like to paint like an Italian race car driver—I watch where I'm going and I don't care what's behind me!

Resources

On the DVD

- Artist Gallery
- Tutorial: Eye Enhancements
- Image Gallery Photo Credits
- General Notes on Art Theory
- Custom Photoshop CS5 Retouching Brushes
- Additional Learning Resources

Links

- http://www.janeconner-ziser.com/janecz/Welcome.html

JANE CONNER-ZISER

Education

I've studied fine art since I was 7 years old through schools, private classes, books, and seminars. I've been in the photography and retouching business for more than 30 years, digital for more than 20. I've studied with the best photographers in the world plus developed my own style and techniques.

Awards and Career Highlights

Craftsman Photographer, Professional Photographers of America, Florida Professional Photographers Service Award, Canon Print Master, Corel Painter Master, Cochair for the Digital and Advanced Imaging Group for the Professional Photographers of America

JANE CONNER-ZISER

Gallery

"Windswept."

"Legacy of My Sister."

"Wonderland."

JANE CONNER-ZISER

"Afternoon Delight."

"Casey & Hunter."

"Beach Ballerinas."

"King's Secret."

"Summer Rose."

FINE ART PHOTOGRAPHY

"Carnivalle."

"Never Forget How to Fly."

H

Z

License Agreement/Notice of Limited Warranty

By opening the sealed disc container in this book, you agree to the following terms and conditions. If, upon reading the following license agreement and notice of limited warranty, you cannot agree to the terms and conditions set forth, return the unused book with unopened disc to the place where you purchased it for a refund.

License:

The enclosed software is copyrighted by the copyright holder(s) indicated on the software disc. You are licensed to copy the software onto a single computer for use by a single user and to a backup disc. You may not reproduce, make copies, or distribute copies or rent or lease the software in whole or in part, except with written permission of the copyright holder(s). You may transfer the enclosed disc only together with this license, and only if you destroy all other copies of the software and the transferee agrees to the terms of the license. You may not decompile, reverse assemble, or reverse engineer the software.

Notice of Limited Warranty:

The enclosed disc is warranted by Course Technology to be free of physical defects in materials and workmanship for a period of sixty (60) days from end user's purchase of the book/disc combination. During the sixty-day term of the limited warranty, Course Technology will provide a replacement disc upon the return of a defective disc.

Limited Liability:

THE SOLE REMEDY FOR BREACH OF THIS LIMITED WARRANTY SHALL CONSIST ENTIRELY OF REPLACEMENT OF THE DEFECTIVE DISC. IN NO EVENT SHALL COURSE TECHNOLOGY OR THE AUTHOR BE LIABLE FOR ANY OTHER DAMAGES, INCLUDING LOSS OR CORRUPTION OF DATA, CHANGES IN THE FUNCTIONAL CHARACTERISTICS OF THE HARDWARE OR OPERATING SYSTEM, DELETERIOUS INTERACTION WITH OTHER SOFTWARE, OR ANY OTHER SPECIAL, INCIDENTAL, OR CONSEQUENTIAL DAMAGES THAT MAY ARISE, EVEN IF COURSE TECHNOLOGY AND/OR THE AUTHOR HAS PREVIOUSLY BEEN NOTIFIED THAT THE POSSIBILITY OF SUCH DAMAGES EXISTS.

Disclaimer of Warranties:

COURSE TECHNOLOGY AND THE AUTHOR SPECIFICALLY DISCLAIM ANY AND ALL OTHER WARRANTIES, EITHER EXPRESS OR IMPLIED, INCLUDING WARRANTIES OF MERCHANTABILITY, SUITABILITY TO A PARTICULAR TASK OR PURPOSE, OR FREEDOM FROM ERRORS. SOME STATES DO NOT ALLOW FOR EXCLUSION OF IMPLIED WARRANTIES OR LIMITATION OF INCIDENTAL OR CONSEQUENTIAL DAMAGES, SO THESE LIMITATIONS MIGHT NOT APPLY TO YOU.

Other:

This Agreement is governed by the laws of the State of Massachusetts without regard to choice of law principles. The United Convention of Contracts for the International Sale of Goods is specifically disclaimed. This Agreement constitutes the entire agreement between you and Course Technology regarding use of the software.